GOD,
HOW MUCH
LONGER?

GOD, HOW MUCH LONGER?

Learning to Trust God's Timing in Your Life

ROBERT STOFEL

LIFE JOURNEY®
Bringing Home the Message for Life

COOK COMMUNICATIONS MINISTRIES
Colorado Springs, Colorado • Paris, Ontario
KINGSWAY COMMUNICATIONS LTD
Eastbourne, England

Life Journey® is an imprint of
Cook Communications Ministries, Colorado Springs, CO 80918
Cook Communications, Paris, Ontario
Kingsway Communications, Eastbourne, England

GOD, HOW MUCH LONGER?
© 2005 by Robert Stofel

First Printing, 2005
Printed in the United States of America

Cover Design: TrueBlue Design/Sandy Flewelling
Cover Photo:- ©Picturequest
Inter Road Sign Designs: TrueBlue Design/Sandy Flewelling

1 2 3 4 5 6 7 8 9 10 Printing/Year 10 09 08 07 06 05

ISBN 0781442001

THIS BOOK IS LOVINGLY DEDICATED
TO THE MEMORY OF

GWEN WHITEHURST HODGES

AND YOU AND I ARE TRAVELERS ALONG THAT ROAD
WHETHER WE THINK OF IT THAT WAY OR NOT,
TRAVELING FROM THE UNKNOWN TO THE KNOWN.
—FREDERICK BUECHNER, *THE MAGNIFICENT DEFEAT*

Contents

ACKNOWLEDGMENTS

Thank you, Mary McNeil, for your encouragement and determination in getting this book published, and to the rest of the crew at Cook Communications Ministries for their meticulous work.

Thanks to Roy Clarke for guidance and wisdom. You cleared the clutter and provided strength and depth. You always reveal Christ.

Thanks to Armin Sommer for offering theological guidance.

Thanks to my wife, Jill, who lets me write about her in a zany, comical way. She's been with me since high school and without me during most of the writing of this book. Thanks for your love and understanding—you've made me a better man and father.

Thanks to Blair and Sloan, my daughters, who sigh only every now and then when they wind up in an illustration.

Thanks to Mom and Nick for their love and encouragement.

Thanks to Hickory Hills Community Church. You've supported me with prayer and much love. It's an honor to shepherd you.

Thanks to my friends Todd and Sheri Hutchison, who listen when I need them and never judge me.

Thanks to Cinda Wales, Kaye Waller, Kathy Winton, Martha Marks, and Kathy DeLancey for helping me get the word out about my books.

Thanks to my two pastors, Bruce Coble and John McLendon, for all the counseling and the ever-increasing love and support.

Thanks to Jared Black, my Timothy. I believe in you!

ONE-WAY TRIP

The Culture of God's Grace

THREE SHIH TZU DOGS attacked me. It happened like this.

My wife, Jill, went to the beach and left me in charge of her beast of a dog, Bono—named after the lead singer of U2. He weighs as much as a child. Boxers look ferocious with their big chests and awkward gait. But they are sweet dogs that require high maintenance. He has to be fed and watered and walked on a daily basis. I'm not a walker. I'll walk to the coffeemaker; that's about it. Jill walks the dog three to four miles on good days. Today there's no Jill and no routine, and he doesn't understand. He doesn't leave me alone until I take him for a walk. He kept putting his snout on my desk, batting his sweet eyes.

"Okay, let's go."

I push away from the desk to retrieve my tennis shoes—a Christmas present two years ago. They are still in the box at the back of my closet. On Christmas, they screamed, "No! Not him!" One look at me and they knew they were doomed to a closet life. Now they seem to be just as happy as Bono, as if to say, "That's it. Keep lacing. Don't stop now."

I have mail to deliver, so I walk the tennis shoes and Bono three blocks to the post office. It's a multitasking walk. But Bono keeps jumping with a slaphappy smile, so I say, "Okay, we'll go around another block."

That was when the three shih tzu dogs attacked. They came out of nowhere. Bono and I were minding our own business, just strolling down the sidewalk beneath an arching hedgerow of trees that thinned against the sky. And the three shih tzus, like MiG fighter planes, crossed the street at full speed—their engines screaming and bodies darting and diving. The first one had no trouble jumping the curb and monkey grass, only to crash on the sidewalk with us. The second one was jumping-challenged. He made it over the curb, but nose-dived into the monkey grass and flipped, landing on his back on the sidewalk and underneath Bono. At that moment, this shih tzu had to be wishing he were a kamikaze—a ball of fire and smoke. Because when he opened his eyes, Bono's snout was touching his.

The third one, being the smartest of the three, stopped in the road while Bono defended himself. The woman who owned the dogs was working in her yard and came running to their rescue, yelling, "GO ON!" But I wasn't about to turn my back until she had her dogs under control—dogs that were yelping in Bono's clutches. Plus, Bono does weigh eighty-five pounds, which is hard to control on a normal day. You add three shih tzus and a defending instinct, and things can get out of control.

The owner yelled and crossed the street in what seemed like slow motion. It was like a movie scene, where the director puts his own dramatic flair into the action. And I waited for her to call off her dogs so I could escape. But by the time the woman joined us on the sidewalk, the fight was decidedly one-sided—Bono-sided. "Bullet the Blue Sky."

She attempted to gather them up in her arms, but they were like greased pigs. They kept slipping away and back to Bono. This was when I caught myself. I *never* said, "You want some of this?!" I *never* encouraged the fight. But I was enjoying my Monday afternoon stroll through the neighborhood. I even made a mental note—*Do this again! Walking can be exhilarating!*

After I made the mental note, and after she got her fighting dogs corralled in her arms, I chuckled. It was over. No one was hurt. Why not find some humor in it? But the woman was humorless. So to save face, I scolded Bono in front of the woman. Because in that moment, I remembered I was a *pastor*, a pastor who lived a block away, a pastor who felt guilt for feeling exhilarated. Sure, it was unfair. Bono wasn't guilty. He was a victim. He wasn't looking for trouble—trouble came to him. But I punished him to save face, to wipe the silly grin off my face. I shifted my guilt to Bono, as if he were the one who'd initiated the fight.

This fight resembles what Christ became for us. Christ became a victim. He wasn't guilty. Your sin and my sin were placed on him, making him the victim of sin. And this idea of victimization startles us. We say, "God? A victim?" But "God made Christ, who never sinned, to be the offering for our sin, so that we could be made right with God through Christ" (2 Cor. 5:21).

Millard Erickson, a noted theologian, wrote, "What is unique about Christ's sacrifice, and very important to keep in mind, is that Christ is both the victim and the priest who offers it."[1] Christ bore our sins and became the "offering for our sin." Our reaction to this determines how we live. It's not a license to sin, nor is it intense guilt. Both are extremes. So how are we supposed to handle guilt and grace?

In Romans 7:24–25, Paul revealed to us his own struggle with this confusing and difficult situation. Here is a good paraphrase: "Oh, what a miserable person I am! Who will free me from this life that is dominated by sin? Thank God! The answer is in Jesus Christ our Lord. So you see how it is: In my mind I really want to obey God's law, but because of my sinful nature I am a slave to sin." Paul acknowledged his depraved condition and surrendered himself to Christ. When we "lay down our arms," we, at last, become happy and guilt free. However, we are never free of true conviction, because conviction is how we know our self-surrender is working. We feel the effects of going our own way, so we repent and turn back to God's way. This is true conviction and noble Christian character. But the false feelings of guilt we have after salvation confuse us. Truth is, after the incident with Bono I felt guilty. Isn't it true that each of us—even when we have experienced Christ's forgiveness—still feels a sense of guilt?

Two kinds of guilt lurk in the world. First, there is true guilt, or "conviction." The conviction we feel after committing a sin is healthy. It has to do with divine judgment. We step away from God's way, and we suffer the consequences. Simply put, God's Spirit convicts us, we repent, and then experience forgiveness.

Then there's false guilt. Paul Tournier described it as the "result of the judgments and suggestions of men."[2] It's the "fear of taboos or of losing the love of others," because of inferiority or poor performance.

Remember the scene in the movie As Good As It Gets, where Jack Nicholson's obsessive character avoids the cracks in the sidewalk? How many of us still "avoid the cracks" because we fear actually breaking our mother's back? Probably no one. But I noticed the cracks on a pastoral visit to the hospital. I noticed them as I took unusually long strides to avoid the seams in the concrete. Unconsciously, I was still operating on learned childhood behavior. My unconscious mind directed my feet. Somewhere inside, this childhood fear still lurks.

Childhood guilt works like the fear of stepping on a crack to break your mother's back. It involves a sense of shame, a sense of wanting to please parents and family members. Tournier described it this way. "All upbringing is a cultivation of the sense of guilt on an intensive scale.... It consists above all in scolding; and all scolding, even if it is only discreet and silent reprobation, suggests the feelings of guilt. 'Are you not ashamed to behave like that?'"[3]

Hide-n-go-seek

"Guilt on an intensive scale" took place at our house on a Tuesday night during a routine bath. Sloan dropped something in the tub that was supposed to be deposited in the toilet. Blair—who was in the bathtub with her—jumped out and screamed, "MOM! You won't believe what Sloan did in the tub!" When their mother came running to find out what all the commotion was about, she scolded Sloan. It was a natural reaction. But Sloan was young, too young to handle such a dramatic scene. Things just moved in the wrong place. She couldn't help it. She didn't understand why everybody was so upset. She stood and looked down at the defiled waters as if to say, *Where did that come from?* Then she realized the severity of her actions. For days, maybe weeks, Sloan would not take a bath. She even formed her first simple sentence.

At bath time, when the bathtub was full of water, she said, "I poop!" She said it over and over: "I poop." And she would not get in the bathtub. Who would blame her? The fear of condemnation was greater than the need to be sanitary. So, every night when it came bath time, Sloan hid. She hid under beds, hid under desks, hid in a closet. She hid because she knew she was a bathwater-defiling, stinking, little two-year-old. And the truth, of course, is that *all* of us have defiled the bathwater. "All of us have sinned and fallen short of God's glory" (Rom. 3:23 CEV). We know this, so we hide. We hide in our addictions. We hide beneath our pride. We hide in our vocation or hobbies. We just don't know how to make the guilt go away.

William James wrote, "The memory of an insult may make us angrier than the insult did when we received it. We are frequently more ashamed of our blunders afterwards than we were at the moment of making them...."[4] Hiding becomes a way to cope with the fact that we don't feel so holy inside. We discover it in popular novels. In *The Five People You Meet in Heaven*, the main character, Eddie, "admitted that some of his life he'd spent hiding from God, and the rest of the time he thought he went unnoticed."[5] It's the cry of the Garden of Eden. "The LORD God called to Adam, 'Where are you?' He replied, 'I heard you, so I hid. I was afraid because I was naked'" (Gen. 3:9–10).

Understanding Guilt and Grace

Repressed guilt becomes extreme when it debilitates our everyday functioning. People with extreme guilt feelings often believe they no longer can receive God's forgiveness. They feel flawed because they've been through a divorce, a bankruptcy, a DUI, or they've lost a job. Or maybe a child gets on drugs and they think they are a bad parent. Usually something happens that throws us off the road of perfection, and we feel broken ... *guilty*. We believe we've destroyed God's plan for our life. We can't comprehend a way back. How can God heal a broken life and make something of it? We convince ourselves he can't. So we repress the guilt, and it eventually resurfaces as anger, fear, and anxiety.[6] Satan gets involved in our shame. He tells us God has abandoned us because *we* first abandoned him. He convinces us that our sin is unforgivable. This is Satan's trap.

How Satan Maintains Power through Guilt

My brother and I loved board games as children. We'd play for hours, especially the game Battleship. My brother was a master player. He had X-ray vision that guided his missiles with laser precision. He demolished my entire fleet and made me do the sounds to match. I'd have to say, "Kaboom! Kablooey!" Then, "You sank my battleship." And as more of my battleships took on water and sank, the madder I got. Then when I couldn't take the humiliation and badgering any longer, I stood and turned the board over, while shouting, "I quit." This was what he was after in the first place. He cared nothing about winning. He wanted me to lose my cool. He loved this moment with a wicked smile. Then he'd yell for Mom.

"Mom, he's doing it again. He's tearing up the Battleship game." The smile never left his face.

Satan induces us to sin the way my brother induced my rage. Then he brings accusations against us and brings us under the condemnation and curse of the law. Millard Erickson believes this is the essence of Satan's power over us.[7] He wants us to sin. Once we do—just as my brother did—he yells, "Look, God, he's tearing up your covenant. Now he's mine again." By doing this, he plants into our mind that we now have to work to get back into the saving graces of God. But no one can work hard enough to be perfect. We attempt perfection and fail, which produces even more guilt. We try even harder and flog our minds with six hundred lashes of remorse. But this causes our repressed feelings of guilt to morph into new sin. Why not? At this point who cares? We're already loaded down with guilt. So what are a few more sins? Women who give in and lose their virginity often say, "I've lost it, so what does it matter now?" They become even more promiscuous. Then they feel guiltier. It's a vicious cycle.

Then we turn to moralistic religion and fall under the same judgment as the Galatians. "But those who depend on the law to make them right with God are under his curse, for the Scriptures say, 'Cursed is everyone who does not observe and obey all these commands that are written in God's Book of the Law'" (Gal. 3:10). Hans Kung, in his book *On Being Christian,* wrote, "This is basically a fatal closed system in which achievement drives man into a perpetual state of dependence from which he thinks he can escape only by new achievements...."[8] This is the reason why we carry excessive guilt. We fall back under a works-based faith, where we can never achieve enough merits to be free from guilt. Then we experience condemnation, meaning we believe Satan's lie and condemn ourselves. Either we hide like Sloan after her bathtub incident, or we run toward sin, throwing caution to the wind.

The way out of the guilt that arises from an achievement-based faith is to know that "there is no condemnation for those who belong to Christ Jesus" (Rom. 8:1). There is only conviction and then repentance. It's the conscious guilt of Romans 7 and the vivid certainty of grace in Romans 8. And it must happen simultaneously!

WHEN THE VICTIM BECOMES THE VICTOR

After Bono and I got home from our walk, I roughed him up a bit.

"Yeah, let 'em bring it on! We got something for 'em, don't we, boy?"

I was exhilarated! I was pumped! It's not every day that you can legally enter a dogfight. You can live your whole life and never know the joy of owning a winning dog. Man! I was pumped! When the victim becomes the victor, there's not a thing a pet detective on Animal Planet can do about it. Nobody's going to arrest you for being a victim. Go to court and tell the judge, "I was just walking down the street, minding my own business, and they attacked."

The judge will hear this and he'll throw it out of court. No one will convict a victim for defending his own hide. So it is with us. Satan can't legally bind us to guilt. We've been set free, but we must not use this freedom as a license to sin. We must use it to become more like Christ, to honor him. Frederick Buechner wrote, "My debt to him is so great that the only way I can approach paying it is by living a life as brave and beautiful as his death."[9] Because when Christ the victim becomes Christ the victor you're along for the ride. The law can't touch you. God has thrown the case against us out of court. You are free from the law. You are free from intensive guilt over sins you committed before you became a Christian. You don't have to ask forgiveness one hundred times for those sins. Forgiven sin is forgotten by God. When we continue to ask forgiveness for the same sin, God has no recollection of it. He has forgotten. "And their sins and iniquities will I remember no more" (Heb. 10:17 KJV). We are the only ones holding ourselves guilty.

But Satan will remind you and hound you. He will say, "Who do you think you are? You aren't a Christian. You did this. You did that. And when you were in high school, you did the unthinkable. Forget

One-Way Trip
• 21 •

about God forgiving you. You are damned." Satan the accuser has been defeated. So why listen? Remember, he's trying to drag you back into bondage. He knows he can't legally accuse you, just as the woman can't legally take me to court for allowing Bono to face his attackers.

There is only one holy enough to take away the sins of the world. There's only one victim, and it's not you, and it's not me. And there's only one victory over sin. It happened at the cross, and it includes *all* who allow Christ to be the victim of their sins and priest over them.

BLASTING THE VERY FOUNDATIONS
OF CHRISTIANITY

Tremors of the Wrong Jesus

THE GREEN FORD TORINO hummed like a hornet beneath the setting sun. We'd passed twenty *See Rock City* signs. Our destination loomed ever closer. The mountains were in view, and my brother and I hadn't asked the "Are we there yet?" question for a good fifty miles. We were dormant doodlebugs in the backseat, hitching a ride on a hornet—destination, Rock City. We were in the last stage of a long haul over lush terrain, weary of semis hustling past us. We'd pumped our arms—imitating the pull of their horns—until we'd developed tennis elbow. And some had responded. Others chewed their gum and kept their hand hot on the CB mic. We'd had our road fun. We'd spotted ten Volkswagen Beetles, counting each one. But that was old now. We only wanted to know one thing: "How much longer?" We wanted to *get there*. We wanted to see Rock City. We were tired of each other. We'd smelled feet and bad breath long enough. We wanted out of the hornet. We wanted to know—

"Mom, how much longer?" It came out before I could stop it. I'd been warned.

She turned this time. We flinched, drawing back into our defensive modes. Our knees shot up. We fell back into the seat, elbows flashing like shields. Then she slapped at us, but mostly hit the back of the seat. She hit my brother first, who whined, "I didn't ask the question. Why are you hitting me?" She then aimed a slap at me. We tried not to laugh, then promised to stay quiet.

By the time we pulled into the Rock City parking lot, we were one big family in love with one another again. The adventure resumed. So did our father's speech about behavior. "I'm only gonna say it once. And there won't be a next time. We'll go home. Is that what y'all want—to go home? ... Don't think I'm lying. You just try me."

Fatman's Squeeze

Mom was right about Rock City. It was nothing but rocks. The first destination was Fatman's Squeeze—a narrow passageway between two boulders. I'd pictured a motorized vise of some sort, something that would open and close, trying to catch people at just the right moment. Then it would squeeze them to smithereens. Buttons would fly. Eyes would pop out. This is when we'd turn our heads.

But it was nothing but two huge rocks. What a letdown. Then I noticed one woman in front of us. She was having a hard time making the pass. She was large, too large. She tried to go through without turning sideways. And I got excited. We finally had some action. I called back to Mom and Dad, who were bringing up the rear. "Hey, y'all, hurry up! You're gonna miss it! A humongous woman is stuck. She's getting the squeeze."

"Shhhh!" Mom scolded me. "How would you like it if some bratty kid were laughing at you because of your weight? I hope she comes back here and sits on you. I won't say a word, not one word."

She smiled to the woman up the trail, who'd eventually turned sideways and worked her way through. It was a narrow escape. No firefighters or special rangers needed. She made it through. We weren't even close.

After Fatman's Squeeze, we had this sinking feeling that things were heading downhill. Then we remembered the seven states.

Twenty miles from Rock City, we'd spotted a sign on a barn that read *See 7 States from Rock City*. Dad said, "All you got to do is drop your coin in the binoculars and *voilà*! Seven states pop into view. You think I'm lying, don't you?"

My brother and I shot each other a look. I knew my brother was about to respond.

"Dad, I don't think you can see seven states from up there. Toot said—"

"Aw, Toot don't know a *toot* about Rock City."

"Yes, he does! He's *been* there. He said you can't see anything but trees."

"And you believe him? I tell you what. You boys don't have a bit of gumption. The boy's never been out of Franklin."

We rode a couple of miles thinking about it. Toot wouldn't lie, would he? It was the first time we'd questioned Toot's authority. He was the oldest and the wisest kid in the neighborhood. But we'd never known him to leave the neighborhood. He was around every day, working or driving his restored '56 Chevy around the square in Franklin. But Dad had a point. We had a choice to make. Who were we to believe—our father or Toot? Would we choose the wise old man in the front seat with long sideburns, listening to "These Boots Were Made for Walking," or the cool kid with long hair and bell-bottom jeans, who listened to Led Zeppelin? It was a question of authority. No doubt about it, Dad was right. But we also understood what Toot was saying. We couldn't make out seven states atop Lookout Mountain, either. After all, there were no dotted lines separating the seven states. Where did the tree line meet the valley, and where did North Carolina butt up against Tennessee? You can't tell from up there. But you can see for miles and miles. And to believe that you could see seven states, you had to go on faith—

faith in the authority of whoever said you could see seven states in the first place.

I see seven states, but I see no way out.

It all boils down to a decision about authority. Everything does. C. S. Lewis wrote, "Ninety-nine per cent of the things you believe are believed on authority. I believe there is such a place as New York. I have not seen it myself. I could not prove by abstract reasoning that there must be such a place. I believe it because reliable people have told me so."[1]

Nowadays, it's confusing. We have popular books and movies telling us that church historians have been wrong. They are trying to rewrite history by questioning authority. They are not denying the existence of Christ, only his divinity. This is a huge deception. Without divinity, Christ becomes just another great teacher, a prophet along the lines of Muhammad and other gurus. It is the same damnable deception we see in many of today's novels and movies that debunk Christ's divinity. "This is the spirit of the antichrist, which you have heard is coming and even now is already in the world" (1 John 4:3 NIV).

Dan Brown, of The Da Vinci Code fame, believes the church fathers lied and perpetuated the wrong history. He asserted in a recent radio interview, "The story in The Da Vinci Code is so well documented, historically, that the only reason it falls under conspiracy is because we all believe a different truth, and my question is: Which is conspiracy? Which version of the truth is actually conspiracy?"[2] How we answer this question will determine what we believe.

Dan Brown believes Constantine corrupted the authority of the church fathers. Brown believes that before Constantine, the church fathers all believed that Christ was a mortal man—only a prophet.[3] It is nothing more than a case against authority. Who are you going to believe? A close study of Brown's claims, and others like his, reveals the flaws in their authority. If Jesus was only a teacher, then he died for nothing. He could have said, "Follow my teachings to discover eternal life." And Jesus' sacrifice on the cross would mean nothing; he died in vain. Millard Erickson compared it to a firefighter answering a three alarm. A house is burning on the west side of town. When the firefighter arrives, he discovers that not only is the house on fire, but the parents are overcome with smoke and unable to go back in for an infant child still within the burning house. So the firefighter rushes in and saves the child. But in the process he loses his life. The child is safe. The firefighter is dead. What an example! It makes front-page news.

Erickson wrote, "But suppose there is no child in the house, and the parents insist that there is no child, and the fireman himself believes that no one is in the house. If he nonetheless rushed into the house and died, would we be impressed by the example, or would we consider it to be a case of foolhardiness?"[4] We would probably blurt out, "What a fool!"

Christ's death was not, after all, for an empty house. He could have told us simply to follow his teachings. But the very Son of God had to die because mankind is powerless to uproot the evil embedded in us by the fall of man in the Garden of Eden. "The sin of this one man, Adam, caused death to rule over us, but all who receive God's wonderful, gracious gift of righteousness will live in triumph over sin and death through this one man, Jesus Christ" (Rom. 5:17). So the "death of Christ is an example, but only if it also is a substitutionary sacrifice."[5] Christ died in our place. He not only provides an example, he also gives us life—having died in our place. "But God showed his great love for us by sending Christ to die for us while we were still sinners. And since we have been made right in God's sight by the blood of Christ, he will certainly save us from God's judgment" (Rom. 5:8–9).

The Bible tells us why Christ's sacrifice for remission of sins is so important to our salvation. A great example could not satisfy God's wrath. Christ's death would in that case be like a firefighter running into a burning building to save no one. Sheer stupidity. There would be nothing redeeming about it. The death of Christ would not have superseded Old Testament faith if it were only an example. The Bible says, "For this reason Christ is the mediator of a new covenant, that those who are called may receive the promised eternal inheritance—now that he has died as a ransom to set them free from the sins committed under the first covenant" (Heb. 9:15 NIV).

Of course, in order to believe in the authority of the Bible, we have to believe the writers were inspired by God. We trust the Bible is telling us the truth the same way we believe in the rudiments of the science of topography. But there are those, like Toot, who believe that the authority of mapmakers is corrupt simply because we can't see the dividing lines marking out the literal borders that distinguish the states. Likewise, there are those, like Dan Brown, who question the authenticity of the Bible because he can't trust the authority of early church fathers. But somewhere—it doesn't matter who we are—we will have to take a leap of faith to believe the authority of any history.

C. S. Lewis wrote,

> Every historical statement in the world is believed on authority. None of us have seen the Norman Conquest or the defeat of the Armada. None of us could prove them by pure logic as you prove a thing in mathematics. We believe them simply because people who did see them have left writings that tell us about them: in fact, on authority. A man who jibbed at authority in other things as some people do in religion would have to be content to know nothing all his life.[6]

If my father was right about being able to see seven states, then why was Toot wrong? Was he wrong because he denied mathematical and topographical evidence? Could it be that he made his determination by the naked eye? Does this mean the authority is wrong?

We live in an era when people regard truth as subjective. There are no absolutes. But if we traveled to Rock City and climbed to the scenic view, what would we see? I might say, "I see seven states because I believe the authorities." And you might say, "I see only trees and valleys. I don't know how you can claim seven states. I see only four." Who is right? Topography or the naked eye?

This is what Dan Brown meant when he asked, "Which conspiracy are you going to believe?" He believes the church fathers were hiding the truth about Jesus' divinity. Which conspiracy are you going to believe? The church fathers or a secret code embedded in a painting? This brings the real argument to the forefront—the divinity of Christ.

What are the consequences if Dan Brown is right, and Jesus was merely a great teacher without divinity? Brown will someday have to stand before God on the merits of his own goodness. Was he good enough? Did he live a righteous life? Did he observe Christ's teachings closely enough? Did he sacrifice enough to follow Jesus' teachings? Isn't Dan Brown taking an enormous risk with his eternity?

What are the consequences if I'm right? I receive eternal life based upon the substitutionary sacrifice of Christ. I won't have to stand trial for my shortcoming. Christ stood trial and died in my place. He conquered death and the grave for me. I live eternally based on Christ's death.

You have to think about this, because this is the choice that Dan Brown and others like him are offering. It has nothing to do with how they interpret history. It has everything to do with how we interpret *Jesus* in history. Their history debacle is a smoke screen meant to throw you off the trail of grace. Without grace, we are bumbling idiots with no hope. Who can keep the law? It is as simple as that question.

Philip Yancey, in his book *What's So Amazing About Grace?*, wrote, "None of us gets paid according to merit, for none of us comes close to satisfying God's requirements for a perfect life. If paid on the basis of fairness, we would all end up in hell."[7] Who wants to shoulder that kind of risk? There has to be divine intervention if we are to escape the wrath of God. "Just as man is destined to die once, and after that to face judgment, so Christ was sacrificed once to take away the sins of many people; and he will appear a second time, not to bear sin, but to bring salvation to those who are waiting for him" (Heb. 9:27–28 NIV).

How to Escape Wrath

My brother and I faced our parents' punishment on a continual basis. We were bad. Very bad. Maybe even brats. We would drive our mom to the tree that stood just outside our back door. "It's got some good switches on it," she'd say right before she made us cut one off. It was true. The branches made good switches. But in my mother's hands the first lash was usually about as bad as being hit with a wet noodle. All my brother and I had to do to get Mom to quit was act like she was killing us. We performed in a manner worthy of an Academy Award. We would thrash around on the living room floor as if bees swarmed in our pants, and when Mom left the room, we'd imitate her and laugh. We deserved every whipping we ever got.

Mom was easy, but when Dad got mad enough to punish you, it was a "whuppin'." That's a Southern expression that means Daddy bypassed Mom's tree and headed straight to the woodpile. My father meant business. I knew this. So one day when he threatened me, I ran across the street to my aunt Louise's house, and I told her I was about to get a whuppin'.

"Is that right, child? What did you do?" Aunt Louise asked.

"I didn't do nothing. I promise."

She knew I was guilty of something, but said, "Come in here to the bathroom and we'll fix this." And she commenced to putting toilet paper down the rear of my pants. "Now go on back over there and take your punishment."

So I did, and my father said, "Boy, don't you ever run from me again." Then he turned me around to administer my punishment and said, "What do you have in your pants?"

"Aunt Louise did it, Daddy! I didn't have nothing to do with it! Aunt Louise did it!"

That is when he did the unexpected. He burst out laughing. I stared at him for a moment, and then realized that I'd escaped a whuppin'! Aunt Louise was a mastermind—the advocate for the weak and guilty! She'd single-handedly warded off a whuppin'.

Aunt Louise is like Jesus. He puts the toilet paper at the back of our souls, absorbing the fury of God's just wrath. Christ's work on the cross took away God's wrath toward mankind. "And since we have been made right in God's sight by the blood of Christ, he will certainly save us from God's judgment" (Rom. 5:9).

This is about as simple as it can be. The rest is up to you. Don't be deceived by conspiracy theories over history and hidden clues in paintings. The choice is not over history but over what we believe about grace and the divinity of Christ. Each of us has to take a leap of faith, no matter which side we are on. Our very existence requires faith. To have faith is to believe that there is more to life than meets the eye. It is to believe in seven states, even though we can't distinguish them from a mountaintop. Faith is a combination of both risk and assurance. "What is faith? It is the confident assurance that what we hope for is going to happen. It is the evidence of things we cannot yet see" (Heb. 11:1). What we hope for with the eyes of faith becomes a certainty, even though we can't see it. As Frederick Buechner has said, "What we need to know, of course, is not that God exists, not just that beyond the steely brightness of the stars there is a cosmic intelligence of some kind that keeps the whole show going, but that there is a God right here in the thick of our day-by-day lives … as we move around down here knee-deep in the fragrant muck and misery and marvel of the world."[8]

No one can know everything with absolute certainty. Just make sure you know the consequences of each side of the argument. Then choose wisely. Your eternity is at stake.

LIFE AT A CROSSROADS

Learning Which Way to Go from Here

BONO, OUR BOXER, RUNS in his sleep. His massive paws dig into a world that is moving rapidly beneath his fluttering eyelids. It's mainly the right front paw that moves. The other three tremble like an addict needing a fix. His breathing is short and rapid. His countenance is as astute as that of a nursing home patient at the bingo table on a Monday night. His jawline droops with innocence.

I'm trying to guess what the terrain of his dream is like. He's probably running the streets of our neighborhood, the way he does when he takes my wife for a run. I imagine he sees the boys who work at the auto detailing shop at the edge of the neighborhood. They smile and yell, "There's my man!" the way my wife says they do as I debrief her while she pats Bono's head and says with a mother-to-baby voice, "Yes, sir. Everybody thinks he's the prettiest dog ever. Yes, they do." He's hot and panting. His tongue drips at the edge of his smile.

Then there's the occasional drive-by Jill tells me about. A motorist will slow down and yell out the window, "Are you walking that dog or is he walking you!" That line is as old as Bono's dreamworld. Jill takes it as a compliment and smiles back. Then there's the stop toward the end of their route. That is where she lets him drink. I know, because

I've been with them. The faucet and the water belong to the auto parts store across from the bank, two blocks out of the neighborhood. They never reprimand Jill and Bono for stealing their water. So he laps while excess water flows into the shrubs.

I don't know his exact location as he runs this daily route in his sleep. I can only see his fluttering eyelids and the way his paws gallop while he lies on the futon in my study—going nowhere but being everywhere. Why can't our dreams be as sweet as Bono's? Why do we fail to relive and savor every moment of our waking hours? Do I have a waking hour worth reliving? Some of us don't believe we do, so we stop dreaming. We stop living and start slumbering through life with no clear direction. We can't decide where life needs to go from here. So we stand still at the crossroads and never get around to following the road that leads to self-employment, or a career as a financial adviser, or becoming a stay-at-home mom, or a full-time writer, or an interior decorator, or the host of *Trading Spaces*, or even the job replacing Martha Stewart. Our feet lull in a puddle of indecision. Then we awaken, like the disciples in the Garden of Gethsemane, and discover that one of the most significant moments of our lives has passed us by because we slumbered through it.

Slobbery, Slumbering Disciples

Jesus charged the disciples to watch and pray while he was in the Garden of Gethsemane. But they slept the moment away. Even though their sleep is a great tragedy, the greater tragedy is what Jesus told them after their third episode of narcolepsy. He said, "Still sleeping? Still resting? Enough! The time has come. I, the Son of Man, am betrayed into the hands of sinners" (Mark 14:41). The moment passed. The stage of history lowered its heavy curtain, the moment irretrievable. They had to live with the consequences of failing to do two little things: watch and pray.

In Jesus' moment of agony and coming to terms with his death on a cross, he sought sympathy from the disciples and the security from a sudden surprise. But they slept when they should have been listening for the sound of sandals in the sand, their eyes fixed on a path through the clump of trees, waiting for the slightest glitter of lanterns, ready to warn Jesus of a sudden attack. But they were defeated by the sandman.

Maybe the disciples' emotions had drained them. The Last Supper confused them. They did not understand why Jesus kept speaking of death. Then Jesus told Peter that he would deny him three times before the rooster crowed. "But Peter insisted emphatically, 'Even if I have to die with you, I will never disown you.' And all the others said the same" (Mark 14:31 NIV). Their emotions were all over the board, and when it came time to watch and pray, they slept.

Most people spend a lifetime doing everything but following their dreams and passions. Most stand around and question life more than act on it. We emphatically say what we are going to do someday, but it's just wishful slumber.

The subtle battle we overlook is to remain awake in moments of significance.

Moments of Graduation

I awakened to one of these moments at my daughter's graduation ceremony. The music started and a rustling in the crowd took place. Parents stood to attention while our graduates streamed down the two aisles, balancing the past and future on their tassels. Mothers dabbed the corners of their eyes. Fathers anxiously scanned the procession, trying to catch a glimpse of their graduates. Then, as the last graduate filed by, the audience turned to square up with the speaker who had made his way to the podium. He spoke about truth, about how truth will set you free, about how happiness is not in material things. He challenged them to seek God. When he had finished, a spattering of parents gave a standing ovation. Then names were called, and graduates crossed a platform, reaching for the hand of a principal that opened and closed with a smile for each one. Then we stood again to watch our scholars march back up the aisles. As the last one marched past, there was a lull. The stage offered no direction. It was a pregnant moment on the verge of birth. We stood, twisting our heads, not knowing what we sought. Then the man who lived across the street from us, the parent of a graduating son, said to everyone and to no one in particular, "What do we do now?"

I knew exactly what he meant. Should we sit again or just dismiss ourselves? But I think he captured the truth of the way we were feeling. We were afraid to accept the fact that our lives would go on after the ceremony. Maybe his whacked Freudian slip was what we were all feeling. "What do we do now?" What will the future hold? Will they be okay? I think that's what kept us standing in the auditorium-lull, the post-ceremony moment. It was a wake-up call where we discovered an irretrievable moment of our own. We couldn't go back to correct our parenting.

After my neighbor's question, I started thinking back to when I took Blair to see Big Bird at the Municipal Auditorium in Nashville. We sat there like two chums, eating popcorn and watching the *Sesame Street* gang dance and sing. Every now and then, when the excitement reached a crescendo, she would glance over at me with a look of energized, utter disbelief on her smiling face. She couldn't believe Big Bird was just yards away, waving to her, smacking his big feet against the floor—laughing. Now, ten short years later, I stood in utter disbelief at her graduation. My child was leaving home for college. Adulthood had dawned on childhood. The past was irretrievable, and I was wide-awake.

The Wake-up Call

Maybe your doctor has given you a wake-up call; you are living and dying. Maybe the divorce papers are sitting on the desk in your study; you are closing the door on a passage of your life. Maybe a child graduated and moved out of the house; now you are trying to fill the silence.

Life is like the transition from class to class in a school.[1] If we fail to master the rudiments of arithmetic before moving to the next level, we will have problems. Every moment of life has its lessons, and there are parts of the lesson we simply cannot retrieve. Just as it is true that we cannot relive our childhood, we cannot reparent our children once they become adults. Nor can we rediscover parts of a marriage when it has been violated by mistrust, because there always seems to be that nagging feeling of betrayal that trips up love's security. This is why we shouldn't fall asleep when those around us need us most. This is why we never make occupations our lover. This is why we keep our distance from addictions. This is why we savor each moment of our children's childhood, not occupying our moments with worry and anxiety.

Jesus was asking the disciples for love and attention. But the disciples wanted Jesus to overthrow the Roman government so their lives would be free. They didn't want to watch and pray. They wanted to usher him in as King, and they lost an opportunity to love.

To be awake in the world is to realize when opportunities to love and be loved are in our grasp. These are moments of great significance.

Diamonds Are Forever

One Christmas I thought I'd stumbled upon a wonderful opportunity to love and be loved. Jill wanted a diamond ring for Christmas. She'd been married for twenty years without one. We were poor, in love, and not so bright when we married. Jill should've taken the "too-poor-to-buy-a-ring" as a sign that hard times were ahead. But she's a good woman; after all, she waited twenty years to get the ring. She pointed into the glass case at the local jewelry store in the mall and asked, "Can I see that one?" The little girl behind the counter, who was wearing enough rings to blur your eyesight, plucked Jill's ring out of the show-case and passed it to her. Jill slipped it onto her finger and held it up to the light. It shimmered and glittered, dispelling twenty years of dark-ness. She turned to me and said, "This is the one."

I tried to steer her to some cubic zirconia. "Who would ever know?" I asked.

She just rolled her eyes at me, as if to say, *I've waited twenty years. Besides, diamonds are forever.*

"Okay, you got it. It's yours, because diamonds are forever."

She smiled.

I smiled back.

Then the manager of the store said, "Why don't you go shop awhile and we'll wrap it."

Jill grabbed my hand as we turned to leave.

There Has Been a Big Mistake, Mr. Stofel

On Christmas morning, Jill's face glowed when I handed her the pack-age. The moment dripped with twenty years of hope. She unwrapped it, darting her eyes back and forth from the package to my gift-giving face. Then a holy hush fell upon the room as she locked her thumb around the lip of the box and opened it ... still no ring. "The box," Jill said with a blank expression, "is empty."

I sprang to my feet and bent over her, peering into the—"Oh, my gosh! You're right. It *is* empty."

The jewelry store had left out the ring, and it was as if someone had stuck a pin in the romance. It sputtered around the room like a bal-loon set free from the lips of a child.

Blair, my oldest daughter, lamented, "This is the saddest thing I've ever seen."

Jill kept darting her eyes back and forth from her prince's face to the empty ring box. I slumped in the chair.

That is when Blair said, with righteous indignation, "We're going to call that manager and get him to open his store, right this minute. Dad, go call him!"

"Whoa! Hang on a minute. Let me think. I can't believe this. There has to be an explanation," I said.

Jill was deflated, injured, completely repulsed and dejected.

"Let me see that box."

"There's nothing in there, Dad. It's empty ... okay?"

Jill was still motionless, stunned, and speechless.

Okay. Time out. Let me stop the scene and let you in on something. I knew about the empty box, because the manager of the jewelry store called the same day I purchased the ring.

"Mr. Stofel, there has been a mistake. We wrapped the box without placing the ring inside."

"You what?"

"You don't have the ring. It's not in the box. We are so sorry about this. One of my employees thought I'd placed the ring in the box, when actually I hadn't. And we have just discovered our mistake."

Back at the jewelry store, the guy apologized profusely. Sweat beaded up on his little round forehead as he stood behind the glass showcase. He shuffled his feet, rebalancing his weight, and said, "I've had a lot of weird stuff happen with customers' jewelry, but this takes the prize. I hope you will forgive us?"

"It's okay, really. Don't worry about it. I'm in the forgiving business. You sell jewelry. I hand out grace and forgiveness."

Then he started telling me about other debacles with customers' orders, and while he was rambling, it came to me like a subliminal message from beyond. I could play this thing to the hilt. Kick it up a notch. Bring in some real romantic tension. Then reveal my surprise.

So I told the jeweler, "I think I can use this to my advantage. Just give me the ring. Don't wrap it. I'm going to play a trick on my wife."

His eyes flickered and a bulb went on in his darkest jewelry store nightmare. "I may have something you can use. I'll be right back." He reappeared with a Christmas ornament dangling from his manicured hand. "I have some of these leftover from last year. It's an ornament that opens." He flipped open the golden egg-shaped ornament, revealing a ring slot, "See?" He shoved it toward me.

"I *do* see. Yes, my man, you are a genius! I will put the ring inside and hang it on the Christmas tree, and when she discovers the empty box, I will tell her to go over to the Christmas tree. Then, *voilà*! What a romantic plan!"

He liked it and wished me glad tidings as I darted out of the store, dissolving into the Christmas rush inside the mall.

The Gift That Wouldn't Give

Back to Christmas morning. "Dad, what do you think happened?"

Feigning ignorance, I tried to appear distraught. "I just don't know, but he gave me a Christmas ornament. Do you think he got mixed up and placed the ring inside the ornament? Go over there and get that ornament."

Jill didn't move, could not move.

So I made my way to the golden egg, and, just like my friendly neighborhood jeweler, I flipped it open and stuck it in Jill's face, and said, "Merry Christmas!"

What a way to give a gift. Magnificent! What a romantic story to tell the grandkids!

Blind Faith

To say the least, it didn't go over so well. She was still bummed, disillusioned, and so mad that my brilliant plan fizzled. What was I thinking? If that jeweler had been a big dummy for leaving it out of the box, then I was his biological replica. I realized my romantic mistake a little too late. I don't recommend that you perform a similar stunt.

Steer clear of such a fiasco. Let the jeweler put the missing ring back in the box. Trust me. Just do it.

What had blinded me to the outcome? How could I not see that this was a bad idea? The desire to be clever and creative caused me to miss an opportunity to love and be loved. It was romance out of focus. I'd give anything to have that moment back. I would change things. But the moment was irretrievable. Gone. Lost to time.

The disciples would sacrifice everything to redeem their discipleship blunder. But it was irretrievable. Gone. A part of Bible history. A missed opportunity to minister to Christ, to pray for him, to watch his back. All Jesus was asking his disciples for was love and attention, which is what the apostle Peter was getting at in 1 Peter 1:13 (NKJV). "Therefore gird up the loins of your mind, be sober, and rest your hope fully upon the grace that is to be brought to you at the revelation of Jesus Christ." Peter admonished his readers to be ready to see God work and to respond to him with instant obedience. To do this we have to be aware of what God is doing in our midst and to be ready for action. It's the same as watching and praying.

Not long ago, two psychologists at York University conducted an experiment in which a man and a woman sat in an office for two minutes, without any reading material or distraction, while they supposedly waited to take part in another academic study. After two minutes, the psychologists revealed the real test by removing them from the office, taking them to a different room. They then asked the man and woman to name as many of the objects in the office as they could remember. This was not a test of memory, but a test of awareness—of the kind and quality of unconscious attention that people pay to the particulars of their environment. The woman—in fact, nearly every woman they tested—was able to recall the name and placement of 70 percent more objects than the men. Malcolm Gladwell wrote in a *New Yorker* article about this experiment: "If you think about it, it was really a test of fashion sense, because, at its root, this is what fashion sense really is—the ability to register and appreciate and remember the details of the way those around you look and dress, and then reinterpret those details and memories yourself."[2]

When it comes to loving Christ, it's about being aware of what he is doing, and then being able to interpret those details and respond to them. This is what the disciples failed to do.

Let Sleeping Dogs Lie

In what areas of your life are you sleeping? Are you missing opportunities to love and be loved because you are making revenge the centerpiece of a failed marriage? Are you sleeping through your children's childhood because your attention is focused on problems at work or at church or in your marriage? Maybe you hate your job. Maybe you've stopped watching and praying for a new one. You've fallen asleep.

Chuck Palahniuk, author of *Fight Club*, discussed this idea that everyone has a passion, and the reason we don't find it is because we've talked ourselves out of it. He summed up passion in this saying, "Don't push the river, it flows." He wrote:

> You could sit here all day and the river is not going to flow you where you want to go. And is it really pushing when you're doing something you love to do? Or is it just in a way surrendering yourself to that thing that you've always wanted to do? I don't see that as pushing the river. I see that as jumping in and letting the river sweep me along rather than clinging to the bank and not doing the thing that I'm dying to do.[3]

There's a lot of truth to the fact that most people spend a lifetime doing everything but what they'd love to do if they were allowed to follow their passion. And sometimes life offers us only one opportunity. So, remember, in a hundred years there will be all new people. Try not to sleep your life away. Don't settle for a mediocre life. Live a life that is worthy to be relived in your dreams, the way Bono relives his tromps through the neighborhood in his.

Christ is looking for those who will love him and be loved by him. So watch and pray. Take a few risks. Stay wide awake. And jump in the river—let it flow.

WHAT'S AROUND THE CORNER?

Handling the Unexpected

MY SECOND SUMMER WORKING at an inner-city mission in Nashville—from out of nowhere a twelve-year-old boy dropped into my life. When I walked in for the morning, he was sitting with his mother in my office. His mother had shoulder-length black hair and wore glasses. She didn't look destitute, but I found out later that she was living in a shelter. She stood when I walked into my office. The boy whipped his head around as if I were a principal and he was in trouble.

"Mr. Stofel, I'm Regina. This is my son, Billy."

I shook her outstretched hand. "What can I do for you?"

"My Billy would like to stay with you for the summer."

"I'm sorry, but this is a ministry for men, not boys."

"I know, but please hear me out. We've driven most of the day to get here." She pulled out his report card. She handed it to me and said, "I can't do anything with him. He won't listen to me, and he refuses to mind me. As you can see, his grades are horrible. I need your help."

I looked the report card over and said, "Well, this is not a center for troubled boys. It's a ministry for crack addicts."

The boy shifted in his seat next to her. He was a spunky, brown-haired, brown-eyed twelve-year-old.

"I know it's not, but you are my only hope. I've tried to get him into summer programs in three states. They're all full." She rubbed his head and then rested her hand on his cheek for a brief moment.

What is wrong with this picture?

"Will you please just keep him for the summer? I'll be back to get him at the end of August." Her eyes were full of a thousand wounds.

The little boy got down on his knees and dug through a tote bag that had clothes, toys, and other things that he'd brought to stay the summer, and there was a black trumpet case as well. Wherever she chose to drop him, he was prepared.

"I don't think we can work that out. I understand your predicament, but, again, this isn't a ministry for boys—only men."

The boy fished a Transformer figure out of the bag and started snapping it, morphing it into a spaceship to fly to another planet—away from her, away from here—I hoped. I leaned forward from my chair and glanced into the bag—building blocks and other types of Tinkertoys. Are you sure this boy is twelve?

"Please, Mr. Stofel. I need your help. Please! Let this be his summer camp."

Summer camp?

I ignored her comment. I got up and opened the filing cabinet behind me. I fumbled through a few files, hoping when I turned around she'd be gone. I heard light crying. It was either a great performance or a true cry for help. I wasn't sure which.

"I need you, Mr. Stofel. I need your help this summer so I won't lose my job. I have to have a job, and I can't go chasing after him this summer. I have no money to send him to some nice camp. I live on a shoestring budget. He can't go unwatched this summer. Please tell me you will watch him."

I shut the filing cabinet, turned to face her, and said, "I'm sorry, really I am, but I can't. So the final answer is ... no." I said it firmly with my eyes accentuating the answer.

"Come on, Billy, let's go," she said.

Billy is my father's name, I thought. I watched him gather up his things and cram them into the overstuffed bag. He picked it up from the floor—struggling with the weight of it.

"Can we go home now?" he asked.

Where will she try to drop him off next? Maybe it'll be worse than this place.

Maybe I was afraid of facing this kid because of the abandonment issues surrounding him. I was him once, in a way, torn by the devices of divorce and chaos. I watched them turn to leave. It was as if I were watching myself leave.

"Hey, listen, I tell you what I'll do. I can't let him stay here, but I'll take him home. He can stay with me for the summer. I have two daughters and a wife who'll make him feel at home," I said in one burst of surrender without taking a breath in between sentences.

She abruptly turned to face me. "You will? You'll watch my Billy for me this summer?"

"Yeah, I'll watch him, but I need you to write a letter giving me guardianship and medical consent."

"I have it right here." She reached into her purse.

She had it "right here"?

I searched his two suitcases, looking for knives, graphic comic books, and so forth. I discarded a few things, but most of it was your usual preteen stuff. He didn't seem shy, mad, angry, or rebellious. He was delighted that I was taking an interest in him. He wanted me to see what belonged to him. Every now and then, trying to impress me, he would pull something out and comment on it.

"Now, Billy, you mind Mr. Stofel. I'll come back and get you in August."

He didn't whimper or beg.

I gave her my phone number. "You can call anytime you'd like. I'll take good care of him. We'll go fishing or something fun like that."

She said good-bye to him again, and we followed her out into the parking lot. She kissed him, got into a long Buick, and backed down the slope in the parking lot. We stood watching as she turned onto Shelby Avenue. He wasn't tearful. He wasn't afraid.

I led him back up the three steps onto the porch, and he said, "Today is my birthday!"

"It is?"

"Yeah, I'm twelve today."

"You're kidding! Well, how about that. We'll have to throw a party," I said.

He smiled. I put my arm around him and announced to the twelve recovering crack addicts under my care that we had a birthday boy on our hands.

They gave him a few high fives and handshakes.

"What'd you get for your birthday?" asked James, one of the recovering crack addicts.

"I got to come here and stay the summer!" His chest poked out, his feet danced slightly.

"You got to come here for your birthday?" I asked. "You mean we are your birthday present?"

"Yep. Mama said I could stay with y'all for the summer."

James shook his head and said, "Well, if that's the case, we definitely have to throw a party."

"I'll run over to the store and get a cake mix, and we'll make him a birthday cake," I volunteered.

They all slapped Billy on the back and sat him down to play Nintendo. I figured while I was out, I would get him a gift. It would be a bona fide party, complete with a cake. I knew he didn't have a Bible because I had searched his stuff, so I would get him one.

At the Christian bookstore, I picked out a nice study Bible. Then I noticed some T-shirts with warring angels screen-printed on the front, along with a Bible verse. I grabbed one. Maybe it would make up for his getting us as a birthday gift. I figured I'd clothe him with the Word and place it in his hand. It couldn't hurt. Maybe osmosis would work.

The recovering addicts sang "Happy Birthday," and I gave him the Bible and T-shirt. He seemed so grateful. He flipped through the Bible. He put the T-shirt over his own shirt, smiled, gave each of us a hug, and then he devoured his cake.

After the party, I called Jill and told her what had transpired. I figured she'd like to know she had a son for the summer. She was shocked at first, and then the idea excited her, especially since we have two girls.

When I took him home, Jill introduced the girls to Billy. Blair, who was thirteen, got me off to the side. "Dad, how did he end up at the Center?"

"His mother dropped him off." I watched him walk around the room, looking at pictures of us. Now, years later, I have a family picture with Billy included. People always want to know who he is and the details of the summer.

"She just left him with you?" Blair had a shocked look on her face, as if I were trying to pull something over on her. "Why did she drop him off?"

I didn't want to tell her that staying at the Center for the summer was his birthday present, so I said, "She needed a break."

"From him?" She craned her neck to look at him. He had an expression on his face like he knew she was talking about him. Then Blair said, "Well, I hope *we* don't wind up needing a break. How long is he staying?"

"Just a couple of months."

Blair was a little jealous to see me with a son for the summer. She and I usually went out on father-daughter dates, and now I had someone who wanted to go camping and fishing.

That night, he wanted to play his trumpet for us. He retrieved it from a tattered black case that looked as if it had made a few trips west on a wagon train. He haphazardly put it together as we watched. Then he blew into it like Louis Armstrong—his lips puckered and his cheeks bulging. We waited for the trumpet's blast, but what we got was the sound of a calf bawling in the middle of a cold field. He dropped the trumpet, smiled nervously, then blew again. This time the walls of politeness fell down. We tried not to laugh. Really, we did. But the sound of it and the intensity on his face set us to howling. Then we caught ourselves, wiped the smiles off our faces, cleared our throats, and thought of abandoned puppies at the animal shelter—anything to bring back a straight face.

"That was great!" Blair, the most caring and sensitive one among us, said.

"I usually do better, but I've gotten a little rusty over the summer break," he said, while placing the trumpet in its case.

"I thought it was wonderful," Jill said with composure.

I was thinking, *I'd hate to hear his school band.*

Me Versus the Manwich

He didn't like my special hamburgers. My daughters love them. But Billy turned his nose up and nibbled around the corner of the bun. So I asked him the next time we were out shopping together what he wanted to eat. He perked up, ran down an aisle, and stopped in front of a display of Manwich cans. He reached for one and held it up. "This is what I want for dinner." He rubbed his stomach and slurped his tongue around his lips. He wanted a Manwich! I was trying to give him my best, but he wanted Sloppy Joe's cousin. I was insulted.

That night we each had a Manwich, and my girls turned up their noses. They loved their father's special hamburgers. A fight erupted over which was the best: Manwich or my special hamburgers. During their argument, I realized how different they were. They were from two different worlds. His ideal meal was a fatherless sandwich called a Manwich. They were from a world of special hamburgers with all the right ingredients.

Trading Up While Trading Down

A couple of weeks after the birthday party, I arrived at the Center with Billy in tow. He liked to go down and play Nintendo with the guys on occasion. When I walked into the Center, I noticed one of the guys had on a T-shirt like Billy's, and I said, "Hey, Billy, he's got a T-shirt like yours, the same angel and verse and everything."

Billy didn't say anything. He ignored the comment, grabbed a Nintendo game controller, and blew up a few things.

I stood staring at the guy, who was also speechless.

Then the guy said, "Oh, yeah, well ... this is his shirt or, I guess I should say ... *was* his shirt. We traded."

"Oh! What did you give him?" I figured I had a right to know.

"A rabbit's foot ... a 'lucky' rabbit's foot."

"Billy, you traded your T-shirt for a 'lucky' rabbit's foot?" I caught my disappointment and gathered up my emotions. I didn't want to embarrass the guy. After all, it wasn't his fault. "Let me see the rabbit's foot."

Billy pulled it out of his pocket and passed it to me while his other hand gripped the controller.

"Yeah, I'd say it's a rabbit's foot, all right." I gave it back and walked off, heading to my office to simmer down. I was thinking, *That had to be the dumbest trade known to man.* But actually, it wasn't. There was one worse than that in Genesis 25. Esau traded his birthright for a pot of stew. Like Esau, maybe Billy thought what he needed in the moment, in the void of having no real family around him, was a lucky rabbit's foot. He knew nothing about God or a warring angel, and he had probably never read a verse from the Bible. Sometimes we make the trade for a lucky rabbit's foot. We love to fret, so we trade the peace of God for it. We love to hold grudges, so we trade God's love for it. We love to lust, so we trade purity for it. And Esau traded his birthright, which involved both material and spiritual blessings, for something that would feed his basic human instincts. I'm Esau more than I care to admit. I'm Billy, too. I have mixed motives. Sometimes I want the lucky rabbit's foot of the world. Give me wealth, then I'll be lucky. Give me good looks, then I'll be loved. Give me justice, and then the sucker who wronged me will have his day.

Why do I trade God's grace for a lucky rabbit's foot?

Maybe I shouldn't be mad at Billy. Ignorance is bliss. Maybe I had to do something more than hope for osmosis to change him. Maybe I should actually show him tough love with forgiveness. I don't know, but I found out he was streetwise and one of the best twelve-year-old con artists in the state—maybe even the country. He could tell the sweetest lie and make you believe every drop of it. The first Sunday I took him to my church in Franklin, Tennessee, he told one of my elders his cat needed food. The elder doled out a crisp ten spot. But there was no cat. Later that summer, when he got in trouble for going to the creek behind our house after I told him not to, I grounded him to his room. While I took a shower, he got out like a stray cow, went down to the creek, and climbed a tree. I corralled him and stuffed him back in his room. That's when I discovered he'd cut the blinds with a pair of scissors. I decided it was time to show him tough love, grounding him for three consecutive weeks.

Thirty minutes after his sentencing, I discovered a sheet of paper shoved under the door. It read, "Please forgive me." Signed, "Billy." I still have it to this day. It reminded me of something. There have been times when I've slid *my own* piece of paper beneath God's door. Maybe you need to do the same today—to say you're sorry, that you need forgiveness. And you will find that God extends forgiveness in the same way I did to Billy. I took him camping later that week with a friend next door. They laughed. They poked the fire with sticks. They spit. They ate. They thought they heard coyotes. They didn't sleep; neither did I. Maybe, just maybe, if anything got through to him that summer, it was how to ask for forgiveness. In some way, I hope you hear it too.

Closed for the Summer

As I thought about Billy, trading that T-shirt for a lucky rabbit's foot, I had to laugh. The boy was brilliant. Lots of kids would rather have a lucky rabbit's foot than a T-shirt. Look at the possibilities. But isn't that what blinds us—the possibilities it never produces? And if you want to talk trades, the greatest is to trade condemnation for grace. Who can ever fathom the depth and the breadth of a trade like that? It's the trade we all yearn for, whether we know it or not. It starts with forgiveness. But we have to *experience* it on some level to know what it is. The sad thing about Esau was that he never got his birthright back. Hebrews says, "Make sure that no one is immoral or godless like Esau. He traded his birthright as the oldest son for a single meal. And afterward, when he wanted his father's blessing, he was rejected. It was too late for repentance, even though he wept bitter tears" (Heb. 12:16–17). There is a time for repentance, and there's a time when it disappears. We are standing in it at this moment. It is here. But that moment will soon be gone, just like the summer. Gone. Like Billy. Gone. Back to the shelter with his mother, back to nowhere in particular. When he got home, if you can call a shelter home, I hope he knew what forgiveness felt like. I hope we were a great birthday present.

I took him home at the end of August, driving into the parking lot of the shelter where they lived. I observed the little apartment he shares with his mother. Just inside the door, a sink, the only sink, hung from the living room wall. A stove and refrigerator separated the two beds in the bedroom. As I stood in that setting, it dawned on me again how different Billy's ways were from my girls'. We missed him as the days turned to winter and the naked trees and the shivering creek went on without him. We missed him when his favorite country songs came on the radio. We missed hearing him sing with gusto. He knew every word and pounded out every beat on my dashboard.

We received a call around Christmas from his mother. She said Billy wanted to stay with us through the holidays. We were excited, and I met his mother halfway, in the parking lot of a McDonald's. He jumped out and handed me his report card. For the first time, he'd made all Cs.

"Well, that's what I call a good report card. I knew you had it in you."

"That's not all," he said. "I have presents for you."

He handed Blair a bulky package that he'd haphazardly wrapped himself. The corners were bloated, the tape loose and ragged. After she opened it, Blair whispered, "Billy, I can't believe you bought me a coat. That was so nice of you." Then she hugged him.

It was a winter coat that he'd found, his mother later told me, by searching through Salvation Army rejects. Why she told us, I'll never know. Maybe she didn't want us thinking she had some money floating around during the holidays.

He handed me a present. I unwrapped it with enthusiasm. I treated it as if one of my own children had given it to me. Inside was a superhero action figure with a broken arm that he'd glued back in place. These were the best he had to give. The only gifts he could afford. As I looked at him—the boy who loved Manwich sandwiches—I realized there was nothing Billy could give me that would make me love him more. He had heard plenty of my sermons that summer. But the most unsettling and poignant message was what I heard through his life. God spoke through a twelve-year-old and said, "Robbie, when will you ever learn: I love your broken heart before me more than the busted-up action figure you have in your hand. All of your righteousness is like the broken arm of a figurine. It's a coat from a secondhand store."

I heard that summer that I couldn't work hard enough to earn God's graces. So tell me, why do I keep bringing my ragged gifts before him? Tell me, why do I trade such love for the lucky rabbit's foot of this world?

WHEN LIFE'S DEMANDS EXCEED OUR LOAD CAPACITY

Where to Go When It All Becomes Too Much

My WIFE WAS IN the backyard crying. We were lounging, enjoying the sunny weather when Jill said, "I miss my sister so much." Then she covered her face and wept. It added a sad rhythm to the noise of birds chirping. Spring was a formidable backdrop. And I could not move. I did not hug her. I did not know what to say, because it was her sister's birthday. Gwen should have been blowing out candles. She should have been opening presents from her two young boys. But she had died on Christmas Day around ten at night. And when Jill cried, I just wanted to make it go away. I wanted to fix the moment. So I said, "It's going to be okay."

It wasn't Shakespeare or Solomon's wisdom. My words were stupid and insensitive. They sounded as if it would not be okay. I wanted to comfort and help carry the load of her sadness, because there are weight limits in sorrow. Most people eventually break down from carrying a heavy load alone. So I wanted to help. But I only understood sayings such as "Big boys don't cry" and "Don't let them see you crying." So I tried to make it go away—quickly. And this was the last thing Jill needed.

Maybe crying serves a greater purpose. Maybe we sow tears in hopes of reaping joy. For Scripture says, "Those who sow in tears will reap with songs of joy" (Ps. 126:5 NIV). The psalmist is encouraging us to believe in the happy ending, the moment when sorrow becomes joy. Perhaps sorrow really does bring us closer to the joyous conclusion.

Mark Twain said that the death of a loved one is like when your house burns down; it takes years to realize the full extent of your loss. I guess that is how Jill feels. The house has burned and every memory in it. There's nothing left but ashes to sort through, like the ashes of playing with Barbie dolls. The charred memory of opening Christmas presents the year they had the flu. I have heard the story so many times it feels like I was there when Clay, their brother, said, "Mom and Dad, I love the present. But can I go throw up now?" And Jill and Gwen followed suit.

The backyard sadness was about being unable to reminisce with her sister. No advice or little secrets or inside jokes. The only thing left is a husband with dwarfed emotions. But of all the things sorrow does, perhaps it is not all bad. Maybe it's the dark tunnel to the brighter future.

The Israelites crawled through a dark tunnel. "By the rivers of Babylon we sat and wept when we remembered Zion. There on the poplars we hung our harps...." (Ps. 137:1–2 NIV). They suffered exile. Grief is much like being in exile. We hang our sadness on the poplars. Our hearts are too heavy for song, and we shut down emotionally. It is like the forty days and nights of the flood. No feelings. No sight. Just the same darkness and rain. Sometimes God closes our emotions into an ark of safety, our emotions battened-down beneath a sense of shock. This is when we say, "I just feel numb." Psychologist Erik Erikson said we emerge by restoring our sense of mastery, which takes place as "we repeat, in ruminations and in endless talk ... experiences that have been too much for us."[1]

I know my wife is sorting through her emotions. She is getting them out. She will move on from this exile. I know she will, like a mother who knows her exhausted child's crying will soon turn into sleeping. If not for the crying, the sleeping would not come. If not for tears, the happy ending would not come. This is why Jesus said, "Come to me, all of you who are weary and burdened, and I will give you rest" (Matt. 11:28 NIV). It's the idea of exchanging our exhaustion for his strength.

The Exiled

The exiled souls by the rivers of Babylon hung up their harps. The weight of them was too much to carry. It exceeded their limit. Joy became impossible. It was the first thing to go in their time of exile. They refused to make music. They desired only to ruminate about the loss of their holy city. Without their holy city, their holy music meant nothing. What a sight it must have been to see those trees filled with harps—the landscape a broken minefield of sorrow. If Jill were a musician, and her only instrument a harp, there would be one hanging in our backyard. In fact, the world would be full of hanging harps because the world is full of sad people. This is a heavy and sad world that exists beside living waters. Jesus says: "Come to me. Hang your harp upon me. Let me carry your burden." But in this verse, we often miss the fact that Jesus is not trying to *force* us into joy. He does not want us to get over it too quickly. He is not saying, "Suck it up. If you really knew me and trusted me, then you would not have the burden in the first place."

It is not a call to deny our sadness. Jesus never falsely removes emotions. The cure is not sleep. Neither is it the cessation of tears. "The world proposes a rest by the removal of a burden. The Redeemer gives rest by giving us the spirit and power to bear the burden.... Christ does not promise a rest of inaction, neither that the thorns shall be converted into roses, nor that the trials of life shall be removed."[2] The musicians did not hurl their harps into the river. They only put them aside to grieve.

Jesus carries our burdens. Our moments are his moments of grief.

We must let him hold our harps. Like a wife asking her husband to hold her purse while she puts on her coat. Valuables are entrusted to the husband. When we exchange our burden for Christ's burden, we entrust to Christ our valuables: our sanity, and our joy. But it does not mean the removal of the burden in our soul; it is help to carry it.

Larry Crabb wrote,

> Beneath the surface of everyone's life, especially the more mature, is an ache that will not go away. It can be ignored, disguised, mislabeled, or submerged by a torrent of activity, but it will not disappear. And for good reason. We were designed to enjoy a better world than this. And until that better world comes along, we will groan for what we do not have. *An aching soul is evidence not of neurosis or spiritual immaturity, but of realism.* (italics his)[3]

Jesus' call for burden unloading is not a removal of the "ache" from our soul. It is the call to partnership: "I will hold your harp so you can put on the garment of sorrow. Now you are free to weep. You can trust me. My burden, my expectation of you in this moment is light. I do not demand from you complete strength. I offer only help."

Hearing this permits us to be sorrowful. We can cry it all out. We don't have to be strong for Christ's sake. He is our strength in a time of weakness. This is why Scripture says, "My power works best in your weakness" (2 Cor. 12:9). He stands beside you. He holds your joy. You have not lost it. He will return it to you. And the moment you turn the corner from sorrow back into a joyful life is the moment you'll hear the music once again. It is not missing. Sorrow is not all you have to live for. Just as Noah saw the sprig in the dove's beak, you will hear the music of your life again. Floods always end. We always emerge from a sense of shock.

Don't be afraid of your emotions when they do surface. Sometimes anger is the first sounding that indicates you are getting close to solid ground. You will feel it. This is normal. But do not be angry with the one closest to you, the one who holds your harp. Do not be suspicious of him. He has not judged you. He has not given you more weight than you can handle. He holds your joy until you can carry it. He has come to make sure that in your sadness you do not lose your most precious possession. Your lost loved ones would want you to be happy, as much as one in sorrow can be. One way to think about this is to ask yourself, "If my lost loved ones were here right now, what would they say to me?"

Getting a Firm Grip on the Harp

When Blair, my older daughter, was six years old, she loved to perform. She would spend hours working up choreography for some song. Then she would present herself at the door of the living room where we sat watching television. She would rock back and forth on the balls of her feet as she held her face up into a pretend spotlight. Then she'd announce the time of the performance. It was always a spur-of-the-moment invitation. We never declined.

We'd straighten our weary bones and make our way to the play-room. Blair would double as both usher and performer. After she'd seated us, she would start the song. She'd dance to "The Lion Sleeps Tonight." And we'd watch. We'd nod when she messed up, as if to say, *Keep going. You are doing fine.* Then she'd finish by belting out the end of the song with one arm above her head and the other stretched toward her toes. And we'd yell, "Bravo!"

We realized she was showing us the way back to the song and dance of our lives. Our minds would hum the background vocals: "A-wimoweh, a-wimoweh, a-wimoweh, a-wimoweh." We would beat out the melodies, lifting our hearts. Likewise, when we turn our focus toward Christ, we see his work on the cross. We witness the joy of his sacrifice. And it calls us back to the harp. It calls us back to his song. Henri Nouwen wrote, "And as we dance, we realize that we don't have to stay on the little spot of our grief, but can step beyond it. We stop centering our lives on ourselves."4 And this will lift the load off our soul.

Rediscovering joy is how we know we are emerging from our time of sorrow. The load gets lighter. Songs find their way onto our lips. It is a sign that we have our hand back on the harp. Maybe you need to refocus your attention. Each of us has something in our life that is beautiful: children, grandchildren, spouse, or some significant other. It makes the pain easier to bear if we can focus more on what we have than on what we've lost. Dr. Arthur Freeman, in his book *Woulda, Coulda, Shoulda: Overcoming Regrets, Mistakes, and Missed Opportunities,* wrote, "Those who disqualify the positive insist upon drawing conclusions only from that part of the evidence that is negative."5 There may seem to be nothing positive in your life right now. But what can you do to honor the memory of your loved one? This may be difficult, but it could give your grief an outlet. My wife chose to participate in the Avon Walk for Breast Cancer, a marathon walk over two days for which she had to raise money for breast cancer research to participate. It enabled her to enter the fight for a cure, and it relieved some of the survivor's guilt. Something like this may help you as well.

The Victim of Sorrow

We serve a Savior who was a "Man of sorrows and acquainted with grief" (Isa. 53:3 NKJV). Jesus faced the horror of the cross. He knew the Father would turn his back. He knew he had to carry the sin of the world. He had to suffer and die. This is why Hebrews 12:2 (NIV) seems to shock us: "Let us fix our eyes on Jesus, the author and perfecter of our faith, who for the joy set before him endured the cross, scorning its shame, and sat down at the right hand of the throne of God."

There was little to be joyful about, unless he thought of you and me. And he did. We were the joy set before him. We were the harp in his tree. We are the reason he got down on his hands and knees and crawled through the darkest moment in history. His Father felt the dagger in his Son's cry: "My God, My God. Why have you forsaken me?" God could have stopped it. But he didn't. He watched the spikes being driven into the hands and feet. He could have called down angels. He could have reached through time with his own hand and stopped history. But he didn't. He turned his back. He had to. And there's no pain greater than God's pain. This is the only way we can accept our own pain.

The Return of the Exiled

The Babylonian exiles eventually returned to their holy city. "The ransomed of the LORD will return. They will enter Zion with singing; everlasting joy will crown their heads. Gladness and joy will overtake them, and sorrow and sighing will flee away" (Isa. 51:11 NIV). In the same respect, I know Jill will have a new song one day. It will start again, just as it did for the children of God. Her sorrow will flee. She will emerge. God's redemption will win out in the end. There will be a happy ending. Jill will see her mother and sister. Then "the saying that is written will come true: 'Death has been swallowed up in victory'" (1 Cor. 15:54 NIV). The weight of sorrow will be felt no more. This is our hope. So we wait patiently while we crawl through the dark tunnel of this world, groping for the other side.

THE STRENGTH AND PATIENCE
TO SEE IT THROUGH

Turning Our Weakness into God's Power to Overcome

THE JOKES STARTED SOMEWHERE around my midthirties, along with the patting and rubbing. My daughters thumped my stomach and said, "What you got in there, Dad?" Then they'd throw back their heads and gurgle laughter in their throats.

Having thus been pushed off the wall of my youth, I found the fall changed my whole culture. I started covering my stomach with long T-shirts that I'd roll around my elbows and stretch out away from my body so they wouldn't look like a tarp thrown over Humpty Dumpty. I even submitted to the "chart"—the one that reveals calories, carbohydrates, fat, and sugar content. Now I stop in front of the cookies on grocery store shelves and read more than the flavors. I consult the chart. Sometimes it's hard to locate. You have to turn the package over and under, trying to find what now controls your life. Then, once you find it, the chart says, *You can't eat this! It's loaded with everything that tastes good. Move it! Go to the sugar-free Jell-O on aisle two. That's all you're getting, buddy! Put this back ... now!* So you scan the audience on aisle two. There's always an audience on whatever aisle you're navigating. They may look like they're minding their own shopping baskets, but they see. They know when the chart has given you a scolding.

Battle of the Bulge

Blair suggested a good diet and maintenance program called *8-Minute Abs.*

"Eight minutes, huh?" I was thinking this might not be too strenuous.

"Yep, just eight minutes a day to having a healthy body."

It sounded easy enough, and Lord knows I needed it. So I grabbed the eject handle on my recliner and catapulted myself onto the floor in front of the TV. Blair inserted the tape in the VCR, pushed the play button, and this was when Jill walked into the room.

"What are you doing?"

"We're doing *8-Minute Abs.*"

She looked down at us and laughed.

"If you're so bad," I shot back, "get down here with us."

So there we lay: a Porsche, a Cadillac, and a Ford LTD—as this demigod materialized on the TV screen. He was barking out commands and counting, "One, two, three. Now take your left elbow and bring your right knee up until they meet."

For the life of me, I couldn't move two parts of my body simultaneously. I looked like a half-dead bug lying on its back, kicking and trying to turn over. Three minutes into the eight, and I couldn't take it any longer. I tried to move my right knee up to my left elbow to stay in time with the demigod, but I was a mound of burning muscles twisted into a sailor's knot. When I tried to move, nothing happened. So I tried again, only to discover that mutiny was taking place on the deck of my spine. Then, inch-by-inch, my body moved. I crawled, fell on my face, crawled some more, inching along, sweating, until I was able to reach for the recliner, my life preserver in a tossing sea. Then I collapsed with a contorted, flushed face—defeated at the Battle of the Bulge.

Jill and Blair started laughing so hard they couldn't finish the workout. Now they call me "Mr. Abs."

Culture Shock

It was culture shock when I stopped frequenting greasy-spoon restaurants and began to "eat healthy." I had to rethink food and diet. I had to exercise to get my weight back under load capacity. Decisions have to be made when life's demands exceed our load capacity. It all becomes too much, so we make new choices. Are we going to allow our schedules to shape our lives, or are we going to allow our lives to dictate our schedules? We can do anything but not everything. We cannot be imprisoned *and* have the freedom to go to the Super Bowl. We cannot be at the same place at the same time. Yet, we try. But choices have to be made.

Harry Emerson Fosdick, in his book *Living Under Tension* wrote: "One of the widest gaps in human experience is the gap between what we say we want to be and our willingness to discipline ourselves to get there."[1] Most of the struggles of life take place as we try to close this gap. Priorities have to be set when it comes to our schedules. This principle is true for both our physical and spiritual health. Every schedule must begin with time allotted to God or we'll run aimlessly. That is why Jesus said, "First things first. Your business is life, not death. Follow me. Pursue life" (Matt. 8:22 MSG).

Erich Fromm wrote: "We are a society of notoriously unhappy people: lonely, anxious, depressed, destructive, dependent—people who are glad when we have killed the time we are trying so hard to save."[2] It's the trap of the *illusory self*—the pursuit of happiness without God. The very thing that Christ said we couldn't do. "And how do you benefit if you gain the whole world but lose your own soul in the process? Is anything worth more than your soul?" (Matt. 16:26). This is the danger in our society today. C. S. Lewis believed we are "trying to let our mind and heart go their own way—centered on money or pleasure or ambition—and hoping, in spite of this, to behave honestly, chastely and humbly."[3] It's the pursuit of self, masked by falsehood. I encountered this tendency in my own home.

Eating Locusts and an Occasional Strip of Beef Jerky

After I fell at the base of my recliner, Jill suggested another diet program called *Dr. Atkins Diet.*

"What can you not eat?" I wondered. It was the right question, because "diets" are all about what you can't have anymore. But this diet sounded fantastic.

Jill said, "You can have bacon and sausage and hamburgers and pork chops...."

"Shoot, that's not a diet, that's suicide!" I said with a smile. "You sure it's not the *Dr. Kevorkian Diet?*" She rolled her eyes, and I continued. "Well, at least you'll look good in the coffin."

I tried it. What did I have to lose but my life? And it was awful! Who wants to eat meat without bread or french fries? Plus, the grocery store shrank in size. There were only two aisles I could choose from— the meat aisle and the pork rinds aisle. (I don't have halitosis. What you smell on my breath is a pork rind.) I discovered that pork rinds have no carbohydrates, and for the first time I understood the challenge of diet and exercise. You can't play at it. You have to give it your lunch and your dessert. And never announce that you are on a diet, because then you'll have weight coaches scrutinizing your every move. They'll say, "I don't think that's on your diet, Mr. Abs." Then they'll place a salad before you, along with ranch dressing, and announce, "This is your diet."

Fosdick believes discipline can be imposed on us from without or we can discipline ourselves within.[4] Discipline from within is the one true way, because discipline forced on us from without usually makes us into frauds. We learn to do as the Pharisees did. They faked it when they didn't have the inner strength or the desire to follow God with their whole hearts.

The bottom line is to ensure you're serious about dieting before groaning through the house about how much weight you need to lose. Because regulations and rules can be imposed by those who are tired of listening to you.

Jill even joined me in my dieting venture. We agreed to hold one another accountable to our daily allowance of carbohydrates and exercise; I seemed to be struggling more than she. Jill never complained even when the only thing on the Atkins diet was a wedge of cheese and salty meat. She never whimpered about a cup of sugar-free Jell-O covered with whipped topping. She ate like a barbarian in the bush. Plus, she found time to walk four miles a day! She was amazing! Then I discovered her secret.

The Right of First Refusal

Jill and I had just finished a salad and a Diet Mountain Dew. She was going to clean up while I took Sloan to a friend's house on my way to the library.

After making it one block, we spotted the mailman, whom Sloan had been waiting for all day. Her school class schedule was due in the mail and she was itching to know her fate. So we returned home and, instead of parking behind the house, we parked in front to make a quick exit after the mailman delivered the mail. We walked through the front door and into the kitchen to discover my wife with another man. She had Mr. Chocolate Yogurt stuffed inside a coffee cup—busted with twenty-one carbohydrates over her daily allowance.

"You're cheating! You BIG FAT CHEATER!"

"I'm not cheating."

"Yes, you are! You can't have that!"

"I'm not on the diet anymore."

"Since when? Since I pulled out of the driveway?"

"No, I haven't been on it in days," she said.

I'd be lying if I told you I was disappointed. I wasn't, because I had been freed. Both of us laughed. We knew that discipline comes first from within. We realized that rules imposed from without lead to a life of hiding our sins. This is the very reason God placed his law in our hearts. "I will give you a new heart and put a new spirit within you; I will take the heart of stone out of your flesh and give you a heart of flesh. I will put My Spirit within you and cause you to walk in My statutes, and you will keep My judgments and do them" (Ezek. 36:26–27 NKJV). The Spirit provides inner discipline. The heart becomes sensitive. It can be moved to shame, to repentance, and to long after God. A heart of flesh doesn't need a thousand blows to be crushed. The outward life obeys God only when the inner life loves his commandments. "If you love me, you will obey what I command. And I will ask the Father, and he will give you another Counselor to be with you forever—the Spirit of truth. The world cannot accept him, because it neither sees him nor knows him. But you know him, for he lives with you and will be in you" (John 14:15–17 NIV).

Our heart of flesh, containing the Spirit of God, is the organizing center and the strength on which we rely. The desire to follow God's law resides here, and when we put first things first, we draw water from this living well before our day begins. We synchronize the gifts and talents God gave us with the power it takes to utilize them. We do this by praying for the Spirit to organize and strengthen our devotion. Most of us spend time praying for our weaknesses and our needs, but forget to pray for God's power to enhance our gifts.

Those who have the gift of administration, for example, never think about asking God to help them organize. It comes naturally. So we go in our strength, believing we have mastered a certain task or area of life, only to experience burnout and exhaustion. And when it happens, we can't figure out why. But gifts need as much prayer as weaknesses, because without the Spirit we run on our own strength. C. S. Lewis wrote, "Now God designed the human machine to run on himself. He himself is the fuel our spirits were designed to burn, or the food our spirits were designed to feed on."[5] Lewis went on to say that when we run our lives on human strength it's the wrong juice. "It seems to start up all right and runs a few yards, and then it breaks down."[6]

Maybe you feel broken. Maybe you have no juice or strength.

Maybe you have forsaken the living water. "For my people have done two evil things: They have forsaken me—the fountain of living water. And they have dug for themselves cracked cisterns that can hold no water at all!" (Jer. 2:13). And anytime we go in our own strength, we dig leaky cisterns that run dry. But there is a source of strength that flows like a river.

Where's the Juice?

Three blocks from my house, the Tennessee River spreads out wide and moist through lowlands and underneath the I-65 bridge. Most days I pass fishermen in their cars with cane poles extending from the side windows as if Granddaddy Long Legs are sitting in the backseat with their legs exposed. They're on their way to their favorite fishing hole. Back to where they probably caught their trophy fish. Back to the mysterious river that conceals its inhabitants.

Praying is much like fishing our favorite place in the river. We go back each day because we know that the mysterious power is found in the River of Life. We don't understand completely what awaits us in the mysterious waters. We just know that we discovered help and strength in its depths. So we go back each day by doing what Jesus said: "Here's what I want you to do: Find a quiet, secluded place so you won't be tempted to role-play before God. Just be there as simply and honestly as you can manage. The focus will shift from you to God, and you will begin to sense his grace" (Matt. 6:6 MSG). This is how we refuel the soul. The juice for the human machine flows from the throne of God to our doorstep, watering down the dry and dusty spots in our souls, toppling and washing away our lack of discipline, affirming that the soul is a well-ordered and reliable place for God's Spirit to reign.

Therefore, start each day with the proper fuel. Pray for God's Spirit. Ask for the inner discipline you need. Then operate in the world as a Christ-powered soul.

WATCH OUT FOR FALLING ROCKS
AND FLYING DEBRIS

How to Keep Your Head on Your Shoulders

MY REDNECK FRIENDS THREW beer cans—even their coolers—over the fence at Talladega Superspeedway in Alabama. They were protesting. You may have seen this on the news. NASCAR finished the race under caution, without giving Dale Earnhardt Jr. a chance to win fair and square. Instead, Jeff Gordon won. And my redneck friends were not happy, so they let it fly. Now, I don't condone their actions. Anything that flies out of the hand of a redneck can kill or at least bruise you. There are only a few things they will throw away beer for, and Dale Earnhardt Jr. is one of them. You should hear the Alabama crowd when Dale Jr. takes the lead, no matter what lap it is. They go nuts ... okay, *we* go nuts. You'd think President Bush was giving the State of the Union address and had called for tax cuts for all beer drinkers. Everyone clambers to their feet and cheers and whistles through the hole where a tooth used to be.

I'll have to admit I'm a NASCAR fan and a Dale Jr. fan. I'm also an anomaly. I don't drink or chew. Some believe being a redneck is hereditary, which means it's not my fault. You see, I didn't choose to be one. It chose me. I was exposed at an early age. I cut my teeth on the backstretch fence at Talladega. We sat on the backstretch because we were poor white trash. I wasn't there the Sunday my friends protested. It was the first time I missed in three years. One year I reversed the order of my church service to be at a race. I preached first, then the praise team finished, while I hunkered on down I-65 to I-20. Two hours. That's it. Just two small fractions of time until you arrive in Mecca.

The only time I've ever wanted to protest was the year an Alabama state trooper confiscated my tickets. It was an innocent mistake. We'd purchased some terrible seats from another redneck. The seats were in the mosh pit where rednecks change identity with every can of beer. We knew this, so we wanted to sell our cheap seats and buy some good tickets. It is common practice among my friends, and it's legal in certain areas of Alabama. So I was standing at the entrance into the grandstands. People were everywhere. It was a sea of colors, each fan wearing the colors of his driver. I was standing on the edge of the main thoroughfare with my two tickets held high above my head when a trooper pulled up on his motorcycle.

He said, "Give me your tickets."

I said, "What?"

"Give me your tickets. You are not allowed to sell them on race property."

"But, Officer, I'm not inside the track." (I didn't realize the idiocy of such a brilliant statement until later.)

"Son, race property begins right out there. If you'd been standing over there, instead of right here, then you'd be legal. You're not, so hand them over."

I took off, ducking underneath burly fans with BO and pushing down Jeff Gordon fans. It was my protest.

Will the Real Redneck Please Stand Up?
Just kidding. The preceding getaway was only a fantasy! I immediately handed the tickets to the nice patrolman and lost $180 in one minute. My friend panicked, because it was thirty minutes until race time and

we had no tickets. What followed was the greatest feat known to rednecks—buying tickets from those who had too many and selling them to those who had none. We got unbelievable seats and even made money that covered the money I lost on the two tickets that were confiscated. Of course, we did it "over there," off race property.

I knew I could get discounted tickets this year. I even drove down by myself—single tickets are cheap. I could justify this nonessential purchase to Jill if it was cost effective. So this year, when a guy tried to sell me a cheap ticket in a not-so-desirable section, I bought it, thinking I would just go in and do some "seat-crashing." That's where you slip into the wrong section and take an empty seat, hoping no one shows up. It happens all the time. Some folks think twice about mingling in with rednecks. So they sell their tickets and walk.

It's easy to play dumb and sit in the wrong seat at a NASCAR event. If anyone says anything, you just get up and say, "Oh, I have your seat. I must be lost.... Sorry." The only problem is, you must first get by the broad-shouldered usher who checks tickets at the gate of each tower. And, this year, getting by the usher was difficult. He was attentive, so I waited. I watched. Then the usher got very involved with this pack of girls, wearing only shorts and bathing suit tops. I'd discovered his weakness. I made my move around them into the Birmingham Towers. Nice view. Right in front of Dale Jr.'s pit stall. I settled into a seat. The next move was to look like I belonged, because the usher kept staring my way, like, *Did I check this guy's ticket?* I knew I needed to do something to keep from looking like a seat-crasher. So I tried to meet the people around me. I said, "Hey, buddy, you a Dale Jr. fan too?" One hundred guys in my section turned to look at me. It was like yelling, "Daddy!" at a Promise Keepers rally. I mean you can spit and hit a hundred Dale Jr. Fans. And after I'd made a few friends, this hardcore Dale Jr. fan walked up to me. He had your Dale Jr. racing gear—T-shirt, hat, cooler, seat cushion, sunglasses. He was ready for war. He was ready to drink Budweiser and yell for his favorite driver. He looked at me and glanced at his ticket. He looked at me, then his ticket. He was trying hard to figure out what was wrong with this picture, while I rummaged through my brown paper sack, looking for my peanut butter sandwich and trying to remain calm.

Finally he said in a gruff voice, "You in my seat, boy!"

In this moment I knew I was an alien in a redneck's seat. I was a stranger in a redneck's world, just as the recipients of Peter's epistle were "aliens and strangers in the world." They were encouraged to "live such good lives among the pagans that, though they accuse you of doing wrong, they may see your good deeds and glorify God on the day he visits us" (1 Peter 2:12 NIV). I stood to give up my seat because I wanted to live a good (and long) life before the pagans. I wanted to live to see my children graduate from college and get married. Life is what I cherished. And if the truth be known, we live in this world more to save our hides than to show our good deeds to the world. Sure, we believe the passage that says, "We live in this world, but we don't act like its people" (2 Cor. 10:3 CEV). But maybe we act more like "its people" than we think. We cheat, lie, and envy. We crash seats at sporting events. We implement dirty business tactics because we are as greedy as the pagans. Sex is selling and we are buying. Often the only difference between the world and us is our church attendance. And I had believed I was closer to God clothed in my deception than he was in his racing gear. I knew he didn't stand a chance in heaven. And for this reason, Jesus told this story:

> To some who were confident of their own righteousness and looked down on everybody else, Jesus told this parable: "Two men went up to the temple to pray, one a Pharisee and the other a tax collector. The Pharisee stood up and prayed about himself: 'God, I thank you that I am not like other men—robbers, evildoers, adulterers—or even like this tax collector. I fast twice a week and give a tenth of all I get.'
>
> "But the tax collector stood at a distance. He would not

even look up to heaven, but beat his breast and said, 'God, have mercy on me, a sinner.'

"I tell you that this man, rather than the other, went home justified before God. For everyone who exalts himself will be humbled, and he who humbles himself will be exalted" (Luke 18:9–14 NIV).

Jesus called a spade a spade. He took on the establishment. Helmut Thielicke wrote, "What kind of strange God is this, who accepts the publican and rejects the Pharisee?"[1] Jesus depicted the religious professional as being far worse than the tax collector he criticized. At least the tax collector knew where he stood before God. This is why he "stood at a distance."

How much closer to God are those who "stand at a distance" than those who sit in the pews? This is the question Jesus asked. If we look down our nose at people and exalt our own righteousness, we may actually be condemning ourselves.

Measuring Up by Looking Down

I wasn't ready for what happened after the redneck said I had his seat. He looked at me for a moment, and said, "Aw, heck, stay where you are. I'll sit down here in this empty seat. I guess I can be nice to a fellow Dale Jr. fan."

I smiled. My life was a gift received back. I even took a long breath. I'd been grafted into the vine of the section, at least until someone came along to uproot him, which never happened. I even made friends with this man who could consume enormous amounts of Budweiser and still cheer for his favorite driver. The distance closed between us, as the gap widened between God and me. I realized how far I'd come from my own darkness, just twenty-two years ago. Now I realized how far I still had to go. This same distance was something the Pharisee thought he'd bridged by his own righteousness. The tax collector understood that in his own power he'd *never* be able to bridge the gap. Both Pharisee and tax collector live in us. At one moment we are feeling self-righteous; in the next we plead for grace "at a distance."

When a man—who didn't know anything about my religious profession—forgave me, I experienced grace. And to do it unto the least of these is one thing, but to have the least of these do something unto you, now therein lies the beauty of grace. It's the realization that you are the neediest and most dishonest in the section. But if you looked at me, eating my peanut butter sandwich and drinking my soft drink, you would have thought I was a sheep among wolves.

This is the deceiving thing about the Pharisee. He wasn't a scoundrel. He paid his tithes. He held down a corporate job. He passed you on the street with dignity, tipping his hat your way. But the Pharisee, as Thielicke said, "measures himself by looking downward when he tries to determine his rank before God.... This kind of self-measurement by looking downward always produces pride."[2] It makes us think we deserve God's favor because we are nothing like the tax collector or the redneck.

Who Was I in That Moment?

If it is true, as Buechner said it is—"if you want to know who you are, watch your feet. Because where your feet take you, that is who you are"[3]—then my feet were telling me in that section, beneath that seat, pointed toward that racetrack, that I'd deceived myself about who I really was. On the surface, I was a seat-crasher. Go a little deeper and I was a Christian professional; still deeper and I was a casual Christian, and still deeper, I was a redneck who felt shameful for every vile sin I'd ever committed. Dig even deeper and I was the little boy clinging to the backstretch fence, eyes popping wide. The grace I found in that moment was human grace, but it went deeper, because where my feet led was back to the person I used to be. I almost added, "But I'm not as bad as this redneck." To say that would have been to commit the sin of the Pharisee. He could not stop measuring himself against the tax collector to see where he stood with God. It's "religion by comparison."

I've worked hard over the years—like the Pharisee—to be better, to silence my flawed humanity that crept up as shame. I hid in ministry, hid in prayer—"Oh, God, I thank you that I am not like I used to be." Somehow, there was comfort in this, but the shame did not subside. So I prayed harder, worked harder, and hid the past I hated. And the trickery of the Devil is to get us to boast as the Pharisee did, then call it prayer. Any time we exalt ourselves, we are trying to convince not only God, but also ourselves that we are better than we really are.

Twenty Years Became You!

At my twenty-year high school reunion, I received the "Most Unusual Career Award." Now tell me what is so unusual about being a pastor? I guess it was unusual because Robbie Stofel, whoever he was back then, was not that any longer. God had changed a rascal, a hustler, a drug addict—a boy who smoked pot on his way to school in the seventh grade. This is what shocked them. This is what they couldn't explain. They couldn't fathom why or how this beak-nosed boy could come out of all of this and have enough gumption to lead sheep. The award seemed more like an apology: "We are sorry for believing God could not change a person this radically." If they can see it, why can't I? I still *feel* like that rascal. Maybe this is good. Of course, it could be bad. I could spend a lifetime standing at a distance.

The difference between the tax collector and the Pharisee is how one understood his wickedness, while the other kept trying to hide it in self-righteousness. We try to silence the inner critic that says, "You don't deserve grace," by trying to earn salvation on our own merits. This is like trying to pay the man back for allowing me to stay in his seat. Money could be involved. And if I felt really shameful, I could make endless trips to the concession stand. Maybe offer a pedicure, and swab a cold cloth across his sweaty forehead while the drivers made their pit stops under the caution flag. The race would eventually be over, and I would not have enjoyed even one lap around the track. In fact, I would have felt guilty if I had gotten past my guilt feelings, because grace is hard to accept. We want to earn it, but "it is the gift of God—not by works, so that no one can boast" (Eph. 2:8–9 NIV).

Why do we feel so compelled to earn our way? Is it because we think of grace as a one-shot deal, and every sin after our initial repentance remains outstanding? Can grace elude us? Thousands of people believe it can. So they drop out of church. This is the danger of standing at a distance, feeling like a lifetime rascal. Eventually, we feel our salvation has eluded us. Now it must be earned, which leads to despair or self-deception the Pharisee modeled in his prayer, "God, I thank you that I am not like other men—robbers, evildoers, adulterers—or even like this tax collector. I fast twice a week and give a tenth of all I get."

We think we can hide our wickedness in our church activity.

Human Strength Failed Even Christ

My newfound racing buddy offered me grace, unlike the Pharisee, who would have blown the whistle and motioned for the broad-shouldered usher. The amazing thing is that my friend believed I should experience grace, even when maybe he could not. Perhaps he'd experienced grace and still hoped for it on some level.

Maybe on a hot Alabama Sunday morning, my buddy went down to the altar in a clapboard country church, knelt on a musty carpet and gave his life to Christ. He knew something had to change. Then maybe he experienced the waters of baptism in some muddy Jordan east of Talladega. Maybe the dirty hands of a bivocational preacher held him beneath the cleansing flood. Maybe that Sunday he swore off Budweiser, only to lapse back into a six-pack after work on Friday. And to face the same preacher with the smell of stale beer on his breath would have seemed like a mockery, so he just stayed away. Who knows? Maybe the hope of experiencing it again resided somewhere deep inside. After all, he would have condemned me as an unworthy seat-crasher. But he didn't. Maybe he felt as Paul did. "I don't understand myself at all, for I really want to do what is right, but I don't do it. Instead, I do the very thing I hate" (Rom. 7:15). And the longer he did what he hated, the more he felt unforgivable.

This is why we "stand at a distance," if we even stand there at all. We know better than to deceive ourselves. We have more respect for truth than to live a lie inside the church. If both parts—the Pharisee and the tax collector—are inside us, then the truth we need is the truth Paul discovered. "Oh, what a miserable person I am! Who will free me from this life that is dominated by sin? Thank God! The answer is in Jesus Christ our Lord" (Rom. 7:24–25).

The Tattoo of Sin

Perseverance is crucial to a believer. It is what drives sanctification, which is the Holy Spirit's work in a believer that makes him holy. "And I am sure that God, who began the good work within you, will continue his work until it is finally finished on that day when Christ Jesus comes back again" (Phil. 1:6). The part we play in God's work is staying the course; developing perseverance. We will stumble and fall. Life has its obstacles. Failure happens. Sin has tattooed us for life. We will never be free of it before heaven, but we can learn to live as overcomers, which we ought not confuse with working out our salvation. This is why Paul said, "I know I am rotten through and through so far as my old sinful nature is concerned. No matter which way I turn, I can't make myself do right. I want to, but I can't" (Rom. 7:18).

Maybe my newfound racing buddy believes grace has eluded him, as grace eludes us *all* the moment we feel we don't deserve it or the moment we feel we don't need it anymore—the way the Pharisee didn't need it. But God is not asking us to perform human works with human strength. No one makes it without God's divine power. Nothing in us merits salvation. So stay the course and say, "Come, Holy Spirit, do a work in me. My soul is open to you." This is the act of turning our problems upward instead of inward. It keeps us from focusing on ourselves, punishing ourselves, the way we think God should.

The key is to allow the grace of God to cleanse our conscience with forgiveness. And when God does, he forgets we even committed the sin. "I—yes, I alone—am the one who blots out your sins for my own sake and will never think of them again" (Isa. 43:25). Forgiven sin is not up for discussion. God says, "I don't know what you are talking about. I do not remember."

In the end it will be the Son's victory over sin and death that will raise my racing buddy, the broad-shouldered usher, the guy inside the state trooper's uniform and polished boots, and you and me. If, in our human weakness, we reach out and take what only Christ can offer— the gift of grace—we walk away like the tax collector, justified and resolved to persevere against the humanness. God will change us by his divine power. "For the grace of God that brings salvation has appeared to all men. It teaches us to say 'No' to ungodliness and worldly passions, and to live self-controlled, upright and godly lives in this present age, while we wait for the blessed hope—the glorious appearing of our great God and Savior, Jesus Christ, who gave himself for us to redeem us from all wickedness and to purify for himself a people that are his very own, eager to do what is good" (Titus 2:11–14 NIV).

STAYING OUT OF THE TOW-AWAY ZONE

Parking Your Faith in the Wrong Spot

THERE WAS A TIME when I parked my faith in the tow-away zone. I felt detached from God. I loathed ministry. I struggled with my calling. Ministering in the midst of all the pain and suffering had taken its toll. I wanted out. I wanted to run. I was wasted and out of patience. I even said to God, "I don't know if I believe in you anymore," only to hear him respond, "That's okay; I still believe in *you*." This is, of course, nothing new for God. Job felt that way. So did Moses. Jonah ran to Tarshish and was swallowed by a whale. And God doesn't get upset at us for parking our faith in the tow-away zone from time to time. Whales can regurgitate. God can get our attention. He can correct our faulty view of him. It was true for Jonah. He thought God was only the God of Israel, and I thought having faith in God meant I'd never doubt.

A doubting preacher is like a garbage man who can't bring himself to throw things away. He needs a new profession. Maybe start a junk store. It wasn't as if I'd become an atheist. I was just experiencing a crisis of faith. I had to clear my mind of a faulty view of God.

At some point, everyone has a crisis of faith, which is simply faith out of focus. The solution begins with enlarging our view of God.

Doubt is sometimes faith that needs an enlargement. Oswald Chambers wrote, "Faith by its very nature must be tried, and the real trial of faith is not that we find it difficult to trust God, but that God's character has to be cleared in our minds."[1]

I wanted a job far away from the artillery fire. I wanted to be back in civilian life, away from the war for souls. I wanted to find my place in the sun, a place where you mind your own business and grunt at co-workers as you drop coins in the lunchroom vending machine. A place where you don't take your work home. So I resigned my church and was on my way out of ministry until God used one man—who had no clue about my inner struggle—to nudge me back toward my dream of being a pastor. It happened when I applied for a job selling heavy industrial equipment. That was the first door that opened.

Here I Stand

It was my first job interview in fifteen years. I didn't really want the job. I applied at the urging of a former parishioner. I went hoping to find nothing. I discovered instead a rust-encrusted metal building in need of a good nose wipe and a long vacation after standing on the corner of Southern progress for more than three decades. Lucky's Industrial Equipment had positioned itself in the heavy industrial equipment market for thirty-six years. Their specialty was an apparatus with a long arm that snatched plastic trash containers from manicured curbs, dumping its contents into the bed of a Sterling truck. I would be selling to municipalities.

Abandoned cars and trucks littered the parking lot. I stuck my truck among them and walked toward the entrance of the building. I opened the front door and entered a reception area that was decorated with a mounted deer head and six trophy bass. The place reeked of ironworks and bologna sandwiches—or was it grease and pickles? I wasn't sure. Stacks of paper, along with randomly thrown blueprints, surrounded an average-looking secretary, minus makeup and exquisite lipstick, divided by the sum of Wrangler jeans and shoulder-length hair, who asked, "Are you here to apply for the sales job?"

"I am."

The secretary handed me a six-page psychobabbled application intended to pry out of me some bad behavior or poor employment history. It consisted of questions underneath questions, underneath questions: "Have you ever shot an employer? Have you ever thought about harming an employer? If you answered yes to question 2, then explain your thought patterns: Would you use a gun or poison? Would you be a sniper or a hostage-taker?"

There's always a wad of words you could construct against your last boss, but why bother? Besides, my last boss was God.

After twenty minutes, I'd inked up a path that led to Mr. Lucky, who retrieved me from the squeaky desk chair that should've been an ominous sign that the company was not a well-oiled machine. I should have yielded to my impulse to stand up, walk out, and leave. But how could I walk out on a man named Mr. Lucky?

I envisioned Mr. Lucky as some intense man with stout nose hair, Johnson grass eyebrows, and big greasy hands from pulling on wrenches. But he was a rather solemn fellow in an Alabama ball cap with the elephant mascot plastered below the word *Alabama*. The bill was flat and pulled down to his eyebrows. His hair protruded from the back of the hat. It was thin, almost downy. No visible blackheads. He looked to be fifty-five; about my height—5'9". He wore glasses with a fake wood-grain frame that shielded entrenched crow's feet. He'd made his money. He'd been lucky. He'd made a good living and found time to hunt and fish. But now, Mr. Lucky was getting older and his luck was running out.

I made a comment about his Alabama hat, and he responded with a politically correct statement: "Oh, I wear Alabama one week and Auburn the next."

I was trying to keep from measuring him or assigning him to some stereotypical social group, but come on! Nobody in the state of Alabama worships at both altars. Somehow, Mr. Lucky was able to be two-faced in a state that judges you by the colors you wear. His comment made me think about my struggle with God. Was God two-faced? Was this the basis of my struggle with doubt? It did seem at the time that God was working both sides of the street. He promises this: "'For I know the plans I have for you,' declares the LORD, 'plans to prosper you and not to harm you, plans to give you hope and a future' (Jer. 29:11 NIV). He also promises, "If you make the LORD your refuge, if you make the Most High your shelter, no evil will conquer you; no plague will come near your dwelling. For he orders his angels to protect you wherever you go" (Ps. 91:9–11).

His promises don't always seem to ring true. When we read these passages, we believe that God means what he says. He will protect us, period. We won't succumb to cancer. We won't have a car wreck, and so forth. But often this is not the case. Do we misunderstand God's protection? Is God two-faced in a world known for its righteousness and evil? Is God offering false hope?

Leslie Weatherhead wrote, "He *allows* human sin, or man would have no real free will. He does not will or intend sin. God is responsible for its possibility, not for its actuality.... But do keep the thought clearly in mind that God's ideal intention, what he *wants*, is health."[2] My struggle came down to this: Does God will the best for us? Why not just make it what he wanted it to be? But, of course, it goes deeper than that. I know. It's hard to understand, so we have to decide that in this world, there will be tribulation. Still, we have to preach something that at times seems so false. It is difficult, if not impossible, to face a family that has suffered a tragedy and say, "God is love. God will bring good out of this."

My doubts in ministry started before I landed on my feet behind a pulpit. Fresh out of college with a psychology degree in my knapsack, I took a job at a ministry in the inner city of Nashville, counseling crack addicts. This is where the unraveling began, because when you are a young counselor, ready to change the world, you quickly discover the underside of suffering, drugs, and meanness. But it is also there that you discover something real, someone who really wants to change. Someone named Ray-Ray.

Ray-Ray was twenty-one years old and resembled Mike Tyson— stocky and scrappy. He looked like he could scuffle with the meanest, but inside this kid was something beautiful. The product of a white mother and a black father, they called him a half-breed, which hurt him. He was looking to be loved. He wanted to fit in. Unfortunately, as often happens, he got mixed up with the wrong crowd and became addicted to crack cocaine. The two of us made progress. He talked. I listened. He wept and bared his soul. I prayed for wisdom. This is one of the beautiful things about a street ministry. You have to be real, or you don't last. You don't have to worry about keeping a critical church member happy so he'll come back to worship next Sunday. These guys are at the brink of death, so they tend to be a little more open than the average church attendee.

This kid was open about his life. He wanted change, and he made it through the year-long curriculum designed for addicts. He got a job, an apartment, and a motorcycle. He was proud of that motorcycle and rode it to the Center to show me. While he was there, he encouraged the other addicts. Lifted their spirits. Here was a guy who had it together. I was happy for him. Proud ... like a father. Then one day, while riding his motorcycle to work, he was struck by a hit-and-run driver. It was random. Evil snuffed his life out in the grease and grime of Second Avenue. Gone. A vapor that still flashes before me. He had so much promise. Why? Tell me why this happened.

Then other things happened. My mother-in-law died. She was the one who had done so much to shape my faith. I can remember the first time I asked her about reading in the Bible. I was eighteen and dumb. I'd never heard of a personal relationship with Christ. I'd never read or heard anything other than the Bible stories you hear as a child. When I asked her where to begin in the Bible, she said, "Start with the book of John." So that night I went home and in my ignorance, discovered that there were actually four books of John—the book of John, then three more called First, Second, and Third John. I read I John 1:9: "But if we confess our sins to him, he is faithful and just to forgive us and to cleanse us from every wrong."

My whole life felt wrong, and that verse forged my faith. I confessed and soon after was baptized. Then she died. It was a dreadful blow to Jill and me. There were others who died—Mike Nelson, a mentor who loved me like his Timothy, died after his body rejected a transplanted liver. Death and pain are confusing, especially to a new believer. It's normal, but I let it get to me. I suffered burnout. I was languishing.

Maybe you're in the same place. Life seems unfair. Friends and family members have died, and you've shoved the pain below the surface. There never seems to be enough time to deal with a crisis the way we should. We just keep functioning until the next crisis, then another, and another. Finally we simply stop functioning and things fall apart. Our relationships get tense. Our health suffers. Our communication with God dies. It feels like God is silent or absent, and our faith feels hollow. We are alone. Then we live on the humpback portion of the question mark, riding it, trying to bridle and tame it, like breaking a wild stallion by the might of our will. But there are some questions we can't answer.

If we are not careful, our unanswered questions will work beneath the surface like the grime that works its way beneath the fingernails of a grave digger as he toils with his shovel. At some point he has to go numb. After all, you can't work with death and feel too many emotions. They taught us in seminary to keep our emotions in check at funerals. We were there for support and comfort only. Emotions should take a backseat. That is wise advice. But your heartache can become bitterness and doubt if left unexamined. Maybe Spurgeon was on to something when he commented on Psalm 91: "It is impossible for any ill to happen to those who are the Lord's beloved. The most crushing calamities can only shorten the journey and hasten their reward. To them, ill is no ill, only good in a mysterious form."[3]

Mystery is an issue. But if I'm going to serve the God of the mystery, then I have to trust him. It's like a man offering an engagement ring to the woman he loves, saying, "I love you." She won't demand proof from her lover. But *we* demand "proof from God—proof that life with him will always be secure." She would be a coercive fool to demand proof. For her to trust the deep surge in her heart and say, "I love you!" is the right response. Then she will begin to wear the ring.[4] We should do the same, because the courage of faith is to trust and love without demanding proof that we will always be secure. This truth has helped me. This is faith. To believe and hope for what we can't see.

That's Just My Luck

Mr. Lucky motioned for me to sit across from him. He glanced quickly at the application, flipping its pages. Then he looked up at me and back at the application, afraid to let his eyes gaze too long into the eyes of a mixed-up ex-preacher. Then he said something fatherly: "Why are you getting out of your field of study?"

I looked up to meet his eyes. Maybe someone finally understood that I was barren without the church. I couldn't tell if he really cared or if his curiosity had gotten the best of him. I was probably the first ex-preacher who had ever applied for a job at his industrial factory.

I knew he was thinking, *How can a guy just walk away from his life's calling?* And even if he was two-faced when it came to Alabama and Auburn, he had convictions about what I was doing seated there in front of him. He thought I was giving up on God too soon. So he said, "Stay in your field. Don't start all over again." Then he added with a smile, "Not at your age."

I stood as if I agreed and said, "Thanks for your time."

He shook my hand and walked me back to the reception area. I turned to my newfound grandfather. He smiled and threw my application in a metal trash can behind the secretary's desk. I pushed through the door back into a world that was different from when I walked in.

I didn't know I was positioning myself for a small miracle or a reinstatement. I never knew God could use a man wearing an Alabama baseball cap. God had welcomed me back into ministry. It was my *Do you want to be made well?* moment. The way it was when Jesus asked the man who had tried unsuccessfully for thirty-eight years to get into the pool of Bethesda. And I wanted to be made well. So I climbed into my truck, resolved to get back to ministry, wherever that might be.

Two weeks after the interview with Mr. Lucky, a church unexpectedly called, and I accepted. The people of Hickory Hills Community Church have changed my life. They've healed my wounded soul. Now I love to stand at the front door of Hickory Hills after every service and shake parishioners' hands, knowing we all shiver before the Lord like the bewildered father of the demon-possessed son, who cried, "I do believe; help me overcome my unbelief!" (Mark 9:24 NIV). For this man, faith was larger than momentary doubt.

Run for the Light

Remember when you were a child trying to get home in the dark after your friends departed for their own houses of light? You dashed or pedaled your bike hard for the light of your mother's kitchen or your father's workshop, because the darkness had unseen dangers that could pounce upon a child. Concentrating on running or pedaling for the light helped to overcome the night's mysterious clanging. So it is with faith. We have to concentrate on light more than darkness. Because faith is the dash toward the light, knowing that the darkness may be there, but it cannot extinguish the light of home.

George Buttrick wrote, "In the faith-doubt tension a man can still make his choice: 'Lord, I believe.'"[5] This is how we overcome doubt. We concentrate on faith. We believe beyond the shadow of doubt.

GETTING INTO POSITION IS ONLY HALF OF IT

How to Stand Strong in Times of Difficulty

ONE SATURDAY, AFTER THE pregame speech, Sloan's soccer coach asked, "Who wants to be goalie?" Sloan had never played the position before, but she thought it would be fun. So she took a risk. Her small oval mouth yelled, "Me! Me! Me!" The coach gave her the nod, and she skipped out to the goal, took her position, and waited for the ball. She kicked the grass. Time passed. The ozone layer depleted. Finally, the ball rolled in her direction. The coach yelled, "Stay in position! When the ball comes, pick it up, Sloan!" The parents yelled, "Stay in position, Sloan!" I yelled, "Just get the ball!"

She waited. She waited. She waited. Then it entered the box, and the coach yelled, "Remember to pick up the ball! Stay in position!" The crowd cheered. I held my breath. Closed one eye. Said the prayer of Jabez backwards, trying to decrease the territory she had to protect. Then a supersonic boom cracked the sky above the field. It came from an opposing team member's foot propelling the ball like a meteorite.

"Get it, Sloan!" the home team sidelines yelled in unison.

She went for it. But she made one mistake. She didn't pick up the ball. She kicked it—right back to the enemy! And *they* kicked it through the goal. The coach was down on his hands and knees with the world in a headlock, and the rest of the parents riddled the field with questions: "Why did she kick it?" "Why didn't she pick it up?" I slouched with my chin on my chest, my hands above me as if a charismatic revival had broken out and I had fallen under acute conviction.

Sloan threw her hands up in frustration. She wanted out of the game. The coach couldn't believe his ears. He'd have a hard time getting someone else to play the position after that reaction. I witnessed one girl begging wildly, "Please don't make me play goalie! Pleeezzz!". The girls know this. They know mothers will get in their cars and talk badly about the goalie. "Why doesn't her dad practice with her?" "That poor girl is pitiful. I could kick the ball better than her ... standing on my thumb!"

The coach asked again, "Do you want to give up goalie?" Sloan hesitated. She chewed it over as if it were a cud. If she said, "I'll stay in the game," she'd have to face her fear. She'd have to pick up the ball. She'd have to hear the parents say in unison, "UGHHHH!"

It would be a risk!

"I'll stay in, Coach!"

Sloan stayed the course and took the risk to play goalie again. She was determined. She bent her spine and placed her hands on her knees. The ball headed her way as her big brown eyes widened with fear.

The coach yelled, "Stay in position!"

The parents yelled, "Pick up the ball!"

It came at her like a Scud missile. She bent down and picked up the ball. She saved a goal. The sidelines erupted in cheers. Parents sprang from their portable chairs and clapped.

"That's it!" the coach cheered, pumping his fist.

The parents yelled, "Way to go, Sloan!"

I strutted around, babbling, "That's my girl! Yes, sir, she belongs to me."

On the playing field, Sloan cradled the ball against her chest and, for a brief moment, she was courageous. She was fearless. She was a champion! She did what goalies have been doing for decades now ... she stayed in position!

What Thirty-eight Years Couldn't Heal

Think of the guy who slumbered on his mat by the pool of Bethesda for thirty-eight years, waiting for an angel to stir the water, staying in position, being courageous.

> Now there is in Jerusalem by the Sheep Gate a pool, which is called in Hebrew, Bethesda, having five porches. In these lay a great multitude of sick people, blind, lame, paralyzed, waiting for the moving of the water. For an angel went down at a certain time into the pool and stirred up the water; then whoever stepped in first, after the stirring of the water, was made well of whatever disease he had. Now a certain man was there who had an infirmity thirty-eight years. When Jesus saw him lying there, and knew that he already had been in that condition a long time, He said to him, "Do you want to be made well?"
>
> The sick man answered Him, "Sir, I have no man to put me into the pool when the water is stirred up; but while I am coming, another steps down before me."
>
> Jesus said to him, "Rise, take up your bed and walk." And immediately the man was made well, took up his bed, and walked. (John 5:2–9 NKJV)

Jesus shook the man's world by saying, in essence, "I know your world from the inside." For thirty-eight years, the cripple lay beside the pool on his back watching the puffy clouds roll by, hoping for the angel. For thirty-eight years, this man positioned himself near the Sheep Gate—a place where sheep were driven into Jerusalem to be sold as sacrificial offerings, a place where wool floated on the water, and the sick lay like a bedsore on the city.

Then, when they least expected it—SWOOSH!—the angel grazed the water with his finger and chaos broke out. The sick and dying came to life and dashed for the pool. Joints popped. Elbows straightened. Knees knocked. Attendants pushed those who were unable. But only the first one in got the prize. Everyone else crawled out defeated and sopping wet with water dripping from their noses, their hopes dashed once again. The man in John 5 had no one to help him into the water. He said to Jesus, "By the time I get there, somebody else is already in."

Why bother? Why torture yourself? Who needs thirty-eight years of rejection and disappointment? I wouldn't do it. I'd get somebody to take me fishing or prop me up on the front porch. At least I could wave at cars like some slaphappy person. But this man wasn't a quitter. He persevered. He may have asked, "God, how much longer?" but he never turned it into an accusation. Bitterness was not in him. It takes character to persevere for thirty-eight years. And when you get lonely, feeling down or even hopeless, please think of him. See his scraggly beard. Look into his weak eyes. Hear his cry as he watches the others being healed, never leaving his position. This is what it means to persevere. "We gladly suffer, because we know that suffering helps us to endure. And endurance builds character, which gives us a hope that will never disappoint us" (Rom. 5:3–5 CEV).

Psychologists believe that optimism is learned. "People who give up easily believe the causes of the bad events that happen to them are permanent."[1] This man never gave up! He was a man of faith. "For a faith like this, waiting is not the falsification of hope," wrote Os Guinness, "but merely the duration between the promise and the fulfillment, between the 'no longer' and the 'not yet.'"[2]

Nothing drops into our laps. Miracles do happen. I'm a believer in miracles. But think of what the crippled man in John 5 must have suffered. He'd seen his share of healed people. The man three elbows down was healed the week before. He flung himself into the water first. The celebration only added to the crippled man's despair. But he never stopped positioning himself at the pool to receive a miracle. What if he had given up the day before Jesus walked by the pool? What if he'd called a cab to go home?

Are you giving up too soon? What if tomorrow your dreams come true?

Remember the children's song "The Itsy-Bitsy Spider"?

The itsy-bitsy spider went up the waterspout.

Down came the rain and washed the spider out.

Out came the sun and dried up all the rain,

And the itsy-bitsy spider went up the spout again.

Arthur Freeman and Rose DeWolf believe we're much like the itsy-bitsy spider. In their book *Woulda, Coulda, Shoulda*, they wrote, "Every time you think you are going to make it up the waterspout, you get washed away. At some point, you conclude that there isn't much point in making the climb again, because it's bound to rain. But think about this: Every time the sun comes out, another opportunity exists for the spider to try again. All that has to happen is to let the rain hold off ... long enough ... just once ... and that bug is going to get where it wants to go. That's the real point of this song."[3] The man in John 5 kept climbing up the waterspout. We never know when the moment will happen. We have to conclude that God has appointed such times. The sick man beside the pool understood appointed times. He'd waited all those years for that "certain time" when the angel would go down to touch the water. This was what kept him beside the pool.

Begging as a Means of Manipulation

When Bono, our boxer, isn't sleeping, he spends 50 percent of his day begging for treats. He knows where we keep them. He knows we don't give out treats just because he stands in front of the cabinet. He knows we have appointed times to hand them out—mornings and bedtime. When we let Bono out at the appointed times, he comes back in and positions himself at the cabinet. Then our appointed times match his positioning and we open the cabinet and give him a treat. If positioning ourselves is the first step, then waiting for the appointed time is the second.

Sometimes we're like Bono. We beg, plead, and whine a little. But God has his appointed times. And we resent it, because it lets us know who is in charge and who holds the plan of our lives. Embracing this truth will free us from impatience, because impatience is simply an expression of doubt. Impatience asks the question, How much longer? It really doesn't believe God has a plan. But God's plan is not a matter of *if*, but *when*.

Do You Want to Be Made Well?

If the first step is to position ourselves and the second is to wait for the appointed time, the third has to be what we make of the new beginning. The change that accompanies the new start may be the hardest part. That is why Jesus asked, "Do you want to be made well?" Barclay said of the question, "It was not so foolish a question as it may sound … if he was cured, he would have to shoulder all the burden of making a living."[4]

The thought of looking for a job must have been frightening. He had no skills. And Jesus was in a sense asking, "Can you welcome a new life?"

Most of us can't. We're forever hanging on to what the past tells us is safe. We live in the light of yesterday, which causes the future to go dark. But this man was in a crisis. He had no reason to go back. Who would want to stay crippled in a vicious cycle of defeat and disappointment? Still, the future was an unknown. At least he knew the shadow of the porch. He understood the life he'd been living. But this new life? He must have had doubts. *Will I survive as a whole man? Can I find a job? Do I really want to be made well?*

Jesus questioned the man in order to make him think. The healing was not the last stage. The man had to go forward, pick up his mat, and walk away. Why take the mat? Forget the stinking thing! Tear it up before the eyes of the witnesses. Give it away. Do anything but carry it with you. The significance of the mat is that we still have to carry the stigma of where we've been. Our past will always be with us, the way it was with Jacob when he limped away from wrestling an angel; the way it was with Noah after he climbed out of the ark and got drunk on homemade wine; the way it remained with Moses after he struck the rock. Moments make a difference. We carry our psychological past with us. Miracles have their mat.

You will have your reputation to carry. You will have habits to break. You will have friendships that need to be broken, not because you are now somehow above them, but because you need to go forward. People can hold you back. But more than anything, Jesus was saying to the man, "You will still face tribulation in this world." A healing will present a different set of problems. The first problem the man faced was violating the Sabbath by carrying his mat. That blasted mat got him busted! I told you he should have left it behind. So much for the happy conclusion! The one who keeps his healing ever before him will be the one who never forgets. And at the end of the day, this is what we all do—we forget. Maybe the mat was to be a reminder of his healing. Who knows? The truth is, we have a tendency to forget. Short memory spans need reminders. That is why Noah received a rainbow.

The Promise of the Rainbow

After the flood, God had to jog Noah's memory. Noah needed a sign, something that was going to help him put the flood behind him. The sun had not taken away the fears of the flood. He was still jumpy. He kept looking skyward, watching the clouds, predicting the weather. Maybe he sat amid the muck and the mold, peering out at the gathering clouds, waiting to see if the rainbow would actually appear. When it did, he crawled out. God gave Noah the rainbow to remind him,

"Noah, it's okay. The rain will always stop." God knew Noah needed a sign, a reminder. Somewhere down the road Noah may have asked, "Did God say there would be another flood, or did he say nevermore?" Then he'd see the rainbow and remember.

We need reminders every day. Did the Lord say I had to work my way to heaven or did he say it was by grace? We tend to live as though performance determines salvation. Living by grace gets cloudy. Facts become fuzzy without a mental metaphor. This is why we take Communion. Jesus said, "Do this in remembrance of me." Communion reminds us he is the way out of our disastrous flood of death. It reminds us to stop beating ourselves up. Anytime we turn life into a continual accusation against ourselves for the bad things we have done—those things we've asked forgiveness for at least a thousand times—we forget the cross. As George A. Gordon said in one of his great sermons, when we worry about our future and fret over what hasn't even happened yet, we forget God knows his world from the inside.[5] If God has an inside view, then it means on some level I have to trust God's view. I have to cross the troubling waters of this world the way Noah had to steer across a flood. The way the man had to carry his mat through a crowd of Pharisees who were more interested in a petty violation than they were a miraculous healing. Helmut Thielicke said rainbows serve as a reminder that God is always stronger than the powers of destruction.[6] God knows the world from the inside.

The "Being Made Well" Life

The "being made well" life is more a journey than a destination. It's an unsure step away from a pool at the Sheep Gate. It's Abraham's dubious flight into the nomadic desert, searching for a city whose builder and maker is God. We won't always know what to do next. And to ask, "God, how much longer?" is to miss the adventure of trusting God. If the crippled man in John 5 had been working from a timetable, he would not have stayed in position for thirty-eight years. The adventure is to discover God in places we never think to look. As we *follow*, the way becomes clear. We see what we need *in the moment*, the way Jacob saw the stairway to heaven. "Then Jacob woke up and said, 'Surely the LORD is in this place, and I wasn't even aware of it'" (Gen. 28:16). God was where Jacob never expected him. God moves in disguised ways.

Our John 5 man believed the angel would touch the water for him one day. This was his hope. This was what he dreamed about on rainy days and cool nights. "When I get healed by the angel ..." he might have said. We're no different. We say, "When I get married ..." or "When I get rich ..." or "When I get a better job, then I'll be happy." We make life a distant happiness. We will never be happy if we can't find it in our present circumstances. There's always something good in life. Then again, the water never moved for this man. His dream did not come true. He had his sights set on the movement of the water in the pool. Then something unexpected happened. In the midst of a sea of faces, Jesus ran his swift glance over the crowd and his eyes rested at last on the ashen face of the man on his mat. Singled out in a crowd. Never did the man in a thousand years see this coming. He expected an angel to stir the water but got a direct touch from the Savior.

Maybe your miracle will come in an unexpected way. Never judge the horizon by the bleakness of the sky. We fix our thoughts on God, not on the way he might deliver us. This is how we must proceed in life. When God redirects our lives we follow the new path with faith, knowing, if we ever veer off his plan, he will be there to retrieve us if we listen. So stay open to the possibility—no matter what the odds. The Holy Spirit "will guide you into all truth. He will not be presenting his own ideas; he will be telling you what he has heard. He will tell you about the future" (John 16:13). Frederick Buechner believes, "Our days are full of nonsense, and yet not, because it is precisely into the nonsense of our days that God speaks to us words of great significance—not words that are written in the stars but words that are written into the raw stuff and nonsense of our days.... And the words that he says, to each of us differently, are be brave ... be merciful ... feed my lambs ... press on toward the goal."[7]

The Spirit knows where we are and where we need to go. We cannot see the way he sees. We cannot know the way he knows. Our spiritual direction hinges on the question, "Do you want to be made well?" We need to hear it repeatedly. We need to listen for it. We need to answer it. We need to hold on when we would love to let go.

Thomas Merton once said, "The real hope is not in something we think we can do, but in God, who is making something good out of it in some way we cannot see."[8]

EVACUATION ROUTE

The Way Out of Our Destructive Tendencies

IN 1981, SOMETHING DIABOLICAL lurked in the South; something worse than leftover Billy Carter's beer; something worse than the evil word *diet*, which Richard Simmons banned from the face of the earth that year. These were only tremors compared to the fiery earthquake that rumbled in Franklin, Tennessee, where a seventeen-year-old girl set my ex-girlfriend on fire.

It happened on a Friday night in the downtown area, where we cruised the town square and blew our horns. Somewhere in the midst of this active traffic sat my ex-girlfriend and her new boyfriend, gazing through the bug-splattered windshield of a brown Ford Pinto. Maybe the boy said, "Let's go eat a Mr. Gatti's pizza," not knowing that my new Christian girlfriend—the homecoming queen, cheerleader, and voted most outstanding senior by her classmates—was working at Mr. Gatti's.

My ex-girlfriend ordered lasagna. That's it. No side orders. Just lasagna. But did she get just lasagna? No! Because a sweet girl named Jill added to the lasagna something that kills romance. She loaded my ex-girlfriend's lasagna with an excessive amount of red pepper, while muttering, "This ought to fire the old girl up." Now, of course, it was not going to kill her, this enormous amount of red pepper. But a girl has to do what a girl has to do. And while the owner of the Ford Pinto inhaled his pizza, my ex kept commenting, "The lasagna here is hot. The lasagna is spicy." But she was hungry, so she ate. Then revenge became heartburn. As they climbed back into the Ford Pinto and sputtered around town my ex became a fire-breathing Godzilla.

Today this is comical. Today Jill asks, "What was I thinking?"

All of us have played our part in revenge. We've hated. We've refused to offer forgiveness. We've sinned willingly. We've written someone off as the apostle Paul wrote off John Mark at the beginning of the second missionary journey. This problem of sin is universal and shows up in places we'd never expect it.

Missionary Hotshot

John Mark was a hotshot. He talked a good game. He'd been nominated the missionary most likely to take the world for God. He was on fire. You could see it in his eyes. The way he talked. The way he listened intently when the apostle Paul described the route they would take on the first missionary journey. He was ready to go. Eager. Zealous. Immature. Still, they made room for John Mark's youthful ideals, figuring he'd calm down once they embarked on the journey. They believed in him. But when the journey wound its way through the treacherous road leading to Asia Minor, John Mark faltered. He whined. He complained about his feet hurting. He couldn't sleep. He missed his mother's cooking. He wanted to go home.

Finally, Paul had heard enough whining. He lit into the boy wonder. He told John Mark to suck it up. Then it happened. John Mark succumbed to his destructive tendencies. He deserted Paul and Barnabas. He went home in a huff. As Paul and Barnabas watched his figure dissolve into the horizon, their conversation may have gone something like this:

"Maybe next time," Barnabas said.

"There won't be a next time for that boy," Paul shot back.

Barnabas said nothing. He kept staring in the direction of John Mark's defection, until finally Paul said, "Let's get moving."

But this was not the last scene for John Mark. When talk started about a second missionary journey, John Mark's name came up.

"Give the boy another shot, Paul. Don't be so rigid. He made a mistake. He went home early. That's all. He didn't commit some gigantic sin."

"No gigantic sin! He left us, Barnabas. He walked out on God. There's no room for cowards in God's army."

"There you go again, talking like you're going to war or something. Paul, it is a missionary journey. Give the boy some room to grow. Maybe this trip is where he'll shine. He learned his lesson."

"I don't know. I don't like the thought of his quitting a second time. We need dedicated people. We need those who will give their all. This boy won't. I just know it. The boy has a yellow streak down his spine wider than the Lake of Galilee. Look at him."

Barnabas glances at John Mark in the distance, skipping rocks across the lake. Paul continues his ranting: "The answer is no! This boy will not humiliate me again. Sorry."

"Well, I'm not going if he can't."

"Fine. Suit yourself." With that, Paul turns to Silas and immediately says, "Let's go."

A Split Decision

Paul and Barnabas's missionary fight ended in a split decision. "Their disagreement was so sharp that they separated. Barnabas took John Mark and sailed for Cyprus. Paul chose Silas. The believers sent them off, entrusting them to the Lord's grace" (Acts 15:39–40).

Paul vehemently refused to give John Mark a second shot. He was hard-nosed. Unbending. No cheap grace here. Paul worked hard for every convert; he felt John Mark should have the same work ethic. And the irony of the verse in Acts 15 is the way it reads: "Paul chose Silas, and the believers sent them off, entrusting them to the Lord's grace" (v. 40). The "Lord's grace" is a strange ending to Paul's very rigid stance on second chances, unless we know ourselves well. We can talk grace but spice up an ex's lasagna. We can peddle forgiveness while being unwilling to forgive. I'm not judging Paul and lauding Barnabas. But there is a division here. Who was right? It seems like cheap grace to allow John Mark to return. Maybe he should teach children's church; then work his way back to being a missionary. But Barnabas didn't feel this way. He was willing to reinstate him on the spot. He was willing to give John Mark room to grow on the job. Yes, he may have stunk up the first missionary journey with defection. Sure, he was spineless. But what if? What if he got it together?

Was Paul too harsh? Did he wound John Mark? Should he have been more forgiving? Was Barnabas a pushover, lacking discipline? Probably the answer lies somewhere in the middle of this missionary split decision. How many shots should our John Marks get? For Paul it was zero. For Barnabas it was one more time. For Christ it was seventy times seven (Matt. 18:22). How do we remedy our own sin? Should we forgive someone else for sinning against us?

Shooting Universal Flames of Sin

Wrong behavior without consequences is dysfunction. It's possible that John Mark was reinstated by Barnabas without learning his lesson. We don't know if he stayed the course with Barnabas on their missionary effort. We know Paul eventually commends John Mark as being worthy of ministry (2 Tim. 4:11). We also know Barnabas and John Mark were cousins (Col. 4:10), which makes us wonder if family dysfunction was involved. Anytime we try to save our sons, our daughters, our loved ones, our spouses from suffering the consequences of their actions, we keep them from transformation. Unexperienced consequences fail to bring about change. God gives second shots, but he doesn't wink at sin. "Don't be misled. Remember that you can't ignore God and get away with it. You will always reap what you sow!" (Gal. 6:7).

But sometimes we have to believe God's redemption is at work. Henri Nouwen wrote, "Patience lets us see the people we meet, the events of the day, and the unfolding history of our times all part of that slow process of growth."[1] Sincere growth takes time. We live with both—sin and holiness. Sometimes sin dominates, sometimes holiness. But there should be more victories than defeats—more faith than doubt, more love than hate. Victory over sin is the goal. Freedom from sin altogether is unrealistic in this world.

We grow in grace with one eye on our present situation and one on our destination. Because, as Henri Nouwen said, "Time becomes not just something to get through or manipulate or manage, but the arena of God's work with us. Whatever happens—good things or bad, pleasant or problematic—we look and ask, 'What might God be doing here?' We see the events of the day as continuing occasions to change the heart."[2]

Paul wanted John Mark's heart to change. Barnabas did too. The problem centered on how to change it. What would be the process? The key is to interpret our sin in the light of redemption. And this was how Barnabas viewed John Mark's setback. He offered a second chance in the light of redemption. But to keep allowing sin to happen repeatedly is to enter into codependency. It's to set ourselves up as this person's god. Rescuing someone is dysfunctional. And John Mark had to suffer the consequences of his actions. The Bible is silent about what happened, but we know ourselves well enough to speculate. Either John Mark realized his failure or Barnabas reinstated him too quickly. Scripture leads us to believe he transformed.

Sometimes we allow loved ones to use us as safety nets. When they're arrested, we bail them out. We save them instead of allowing them to suffer the consequences. We transplant them into our homes.

Then when they fail to change, we make excuses for them. We hide their sins. We cover their hides. But this is not growing in grace. This is dysfunction.

Should we help them? Yes, but don't become the safety net they use every time they fall. Or they will say something like this: "It doesn't matter if I get in trouble; he/she will save me. He/she will bail me out. So who cares? Let's do it!" No consequences. No conscience.

Our wayward loved ones need second chances with tough love. But if you are caught in their cycle of addiction, abuse, or crime, it's time for you to exit. Your help may be keeping them in the cycle. Remember, most wayward loved ones know how to throw a thousand little knives of guilt. They threaten. They cuss. They kick. And when this is not enough, they call in the heavy artillery. They become pitiful. They curl their bottom lip and whimper. And what do they expect the family to do? Relent? Why should their waywardness ruin our lives too? No sane person holds a family hostage. They deal with their own demons without becoming one.

Maybe Barnabas discerned in his cousin John Mark a sense of regret and remorse. And if you detect this in your wayward loved one, then you have a basis for giving him a second or thirty-second try. It means that he is becoming human and leaving behind his thoughts of grandeur.

Thomas Merton believed a Christian will grow in grace by learning how to be truly human. He wrote, "[Holiness] is not a matter of being *less* human, but *more* human than other men. This implies a greater capacity for concern, for suffering, for understanding, for sympathy, and also for humor, for joy, for appreciation of the good and beautiful things of life."[3] We know we've succeeded when our loved one lets down his mask and becomes remorseful, instead of sorry he got caught. He does so because he senses our compassion, compassion that understands the human condition—but also because he wants to be free of evil desires.

The Divine in Our Children

When Sloan's friend stuttered, I wasn't expecting it, even though Jill had warned me.

"The little girl that's coming home with Sloan has a speech impediment."

"Okay, thanks for telling me."

"I just thought I'd prepare you."

Still, it was difficult when I heard her for the first time. I wasn't prepared. It was the sort of speech you'd use while being mugged on a dark street corner. "O–o–o–kay, you c–c–can have my w–w–wallet." It made me want to protect her from the world. I wished I could gather out of thin air the misplaced parts of speech and put them together for her. It broke my heart.

After dinner, I took Sloan and her friend out to rent a movie. We loaded up in the Honda Passport. They sat in the backseat, gibbering preadolescence—boys and boy bands, and so on. And on the way home, they said, "Turn up the radio," so I turned it up. Then they said, "Turn it up some more." So I turned it up some more. Sloan was singing along with Jessica Simpson, and we were thumping down Sixth Avenue like one of those low riders with the bass turned up. We were thumping beneath red lights and as we passed service stations. Then I heard the little girl that stutters yell over the music, "Can I tell you a secret?"

"Sure," Sloan said with eyes of endearment. (I was watching the scene in the rearview mirror.)

I, too, wanted to say, "Sure, tell the secret."

Then the little girl said, "O–o–okay, you c–c–can't tell anyb–b–body, but I've never sung in f–f–front of anyone b–before." It floated through the air and around the car as we passed Carl's Quick Stop.

Why did she want Sloan to know this secret? Why doesn't she sing in front of people?

Maybe when she sings, it's a reverse Mel Tillis. Maybe, instead of bouncing around the SUV like a balloon, her stuttering would become Speedy Gonzales on a pogo stick. I don't know, but Sloan tried to get her to sing. And I was proud of Sloan, because I could tell she was sincere. She was showing her friend divine compassion. She was trying to draw out the shame the little girl felt inside. She was giving her room to be broken. That is hard to find in this world. Maybe it is easier for children. Maybe that is why Jesus said, "I assure you, unless you turn from your sins and become as little children, you will never get into the Kingdom of Heaven" (Matt. 18:3).

And the little girl said, "T–t–that's j–j–just something I c–c–can't do."

The short journey changed us. There was something different about us when we got back, because seeing and hearing her admit her brokenness cast a new atmosphere in our SUV. Our journey to the video rental store became a moment of unforgettable brokenness transformed into holy light. The stutterer became a saint in my eyes, because it's one thing to recognize your weakness, but there's something holy about having the courage to admit it. She didn't fear the darkness she felt. That is bravery, even sainthood—to live with the tension of holiness and brokenness.

So let us still our throbbing anxiety. Let us trust our wayward sons and daughters to his redemptive power.

KEEP OFF!

The Dead Center of Self

ORANGE BEACH, ALABAMA, IS a haven. Some would say "for rednecks." Yet that would not be entirely true. The truth is, Panama City Beach, Florida, is home to the Redneck Confederation of the Inconsiderate. Every now and then, though, a few slither westward to the easternmost tip of our great state. This particular day, it seemed that some of them had found a home in the condo above our heads. Wild beasts were corralled up there. They had two spittoons that sat out on the deck where they smoked cigarettes and drank coffee. The beasts could smell the ocean. They had their buckets and shovels looped inside their claws, waiting to be released into the great outdoors from whence they came. But this usually didn't happen until noon. So the Stofels, those saints who dwelled below, had to wait it out. We had to rise early and wonder what was taking place above our heads. The scrubbing noise woke me first. It sounded like a peg leg scraping across the deck of a pirate ship. It didn't happen just once; it sounded like a pirate ship struggling in a nor'easter with crippled pirates traveling from stem to stern. It was a free-for-all—as if Ted Nugent's kids were hunting and killing wild boar in the space above us.

I spotted them one midday. There were going out. I was headed in.

We passed each other on the wooden ramp that jutted down to the beach. They looked normal and were even pulling a grandfather along. Each wore sandals and a swimsuit. They were punch-drunk in love with the beach they saw beyond their tiny feet. Every kid is. But the mom of this gypsy band of tromping rednecks made them take off their shoes before they stepped on the beach. I thought that strange, seeing that the sand was about 115 degrees above blistering. Maybe it was her way of getting them to sit still. "I'll scorch their little feet, and then tonight I'll dare them to run around the seafood buffet at Hazel's Restaurant. This will keep them in their seats. This will keep them from jumping off the bed." And in that moment, I praised her. "What a great mom!"

I rose early the next morning to write. I wanted to power my way through a few chapters while on vacation. I was looking forward to an early morning of silent, uneventful creative writing. Then it started again like a rowdy circus act. I thought I might be onto something. Maybe a circus was practicing above our heads. I could visualize elephants balanced on each other's backs. I could hear them shuffling their feet. Then there was the dramatic flight of the trapeze artist sailing in bewildered silence before his trapeze partner caught him. Next a helmeted daredevil shot out of a cannon. He landed above my head with a thud, and I thought about calling 911. But the little rug rats would be standing, bowing to each end of the big tent by the time the 911 operator took down the address. Act III would be a parade of freaks. I could hear the three-legged midget walking on my head. Then silence again. I almost clapped. Then three flamethrowers, swallowing torches and blowing red flames, walked across the ceiling. Scratch that. No circus act with flamethrowers; that was fantasy mixed with reality. What I thought were flamethrowers were really Jill, Sloan, and one of Sloan's friends, Sarah. They arose from their slumber exuding bad breath and wanting to know how much longer I was going to sit below this craziness. How long before I took matters into my own hands, climbed the steps, knocked on their door, and demanded, "QUIET!"

I showed them the broomstick covered with drywall dust, the same one I'd been banging on the ceiling, hoping it would communicate, "Shut up! Be quiet up there!" But it did not. The circus continued. My actions did not work. But there was no way I was going to climb those steps and demand a halt, not these days. I could get shot, or worse. I've watched my share of *Cops*. I know how evil works. Why bother?

I sat, unmoving, committed to no action other than the broom method. But as I observed their countenances, I saw my family's R&R deteriorating. It was time to act. "God, how much longer before you make them leave?" I whined plaintively. "Don't they have an appointment at the podiatrist? Send them to *Smallville*. Make it a rerun."

God, How Much Longer?

We tend to lay on God what we don't have the guts to do for ourselves. We pray prayers of bewitching. "God, do this." "God, curse that." "God, how much longer?" We say all of this as if God is the great grandfather in the sky, waiting to set the world aright at our first twinge of discomfort. C. S. Lewis wrote, "We want, in fact, not so much a Father in Heaven as a Grandfather in heaven—a senile benevolence who, as they say, 'liked to see young people enjoying themselves,' and whose plan for the universe was simply that it might be truly said at the end of each day, 'a good time was had by all.'"[1]

I somehow believed this. It was "my" trip to do "God's" writing, so why didn't God send out the message, "Stay quiet; Robert is writing"? But we don't always get what we want. Just ask James and John about accommodation problems. A Samaritan village had refused lodging for Jesus, and the boys shouted, "Lord, should we order down fire from heaven to burn them up?"[2] It seems at first glance that James and John are pyromaniacs. Fire is their answer. Judgment is the cure for their inconvenience. And isn't this true for us all? We judge the slow guy at the red light with a blast of our horn. We judge the noisy neighbors upstairs as backwoods rednecks that deserve to be tossed out on their trucker wallets. But Jesus said, "You do not know what ... spirit you are of" (Luke 9:55 NKJV). If any sentence of Jesus' echoes down to our time, it is this one.

We have lost touch with "what spirit we are of." We believe anything that rumbles into our dreams and messes up our peace is ungodly and deserves annihilation. We stand at the center of our own universe, demanding God follow *our* plotlines. Besides, my ability to concentrate is more important than the fun the kids above my head are having. John Calvin understood this when he said, "There is nobody who does not imagine that he is really better than others."[3] When we stop to ask ourselves what spirit we are of, it changes the way we relate to the world. Barclay wrote, "Even if a man be utterly mistaken, we must never regard him as an enemy to be destroyed but as a strayed friend to be recovered by love."[4]

Selfish pursuit demands happiness on our own terms. If we fail to get it, we get the broom handle and stab the floor of heaven saying, God, what's going on up there? Can't you see you've allowed things to deviate from my plans? How much longer will you remain silent? James and John were probably more upset about Jesus' nonviolent approach than they were by a no-vacancy message. They were men of action. They'd dealt with crabby sea captains. They knew about human resource challenges in their fishing business. You have to nip them in the bud. Control people before they control you. It's smart business practice. It's a dog-eat-dog world. You sometimes have to use heavenly force to influence worldly snobbery. This is where they veered off God's plan. They made the focus "getting their way in a Samaritan village."

Maybe you're standing with a broomstick in your hand. Maybe you have been banging the floor of heaven, demanding to know what's going on up there. But nothing is changing. Make sure you check with God for the bigger picture. He may be keeping you from getting involved in a struggle that has nothing to do with his greater purpose. Bitterness and revenge is a bunny trail, a detour, an all-encompassing waste of energy. Get back on mission. Align your life with the greater picture of forgiveness, of humility, of trading your weakness for his strength. Take up your cross and follow him to the hill. Lay down your hatred there. The process of becoming a child of God can be painful because we often don't get our way. We will suffer and cry during the journey. And, as Lewis pointed out, the "trouble is that when it comes to genuine Christian living, fine in quality, radiant in influence, steady in difficult, victorious in temptation, aware of inward resources of spiritual power, we applaud the ideal but we take no pains with the means of reaching it."[5]

The eyes of love are tolerant. The right spirit fixes its eyes on the big picture, which for James and John should have been the crucifixion that was about to take place in Jerusalem. That is what's so beautiful about Jesus' comment that Luke recorded in his gospel. "So they went on to another village" (Luke 9:56). Jesus didn't allow them to get caught up in what they thought they deserved. Ego has no place on the road to the cross. Getting even isn't the right spirit. It *never* is. Something was happening that was bigger than personal treatment. Bible commentator John Nolland identified the greater priority. "What is important is that the journeying continues."[6] Movement is monumental to getting somewhere.

Every follower of Jesus is on a journey to full redemption. That is why being of the wrong spirit is detrimental. It is a wasted moment. Inconvenience is not a reason to fry someone. In our pursuit for contentment and happiness, people are not at our disposal. "If anyone boasts, 'I love God,' and goes right on hating his brother or sister, thinking nothing of it, he is a liar" (1 John 4:20 MSG). How can we love God and hate a fellow traveler? We can't. Our focus on the journey isn't to get somewhere before dark. It's to travel into the darkness without losing our light. It is to grow more in love with both God and people. The arrival time to our destination is up to God. We are to travel in the right spirit with unselfish eyes of love.

A Change of Internal Venue

After asking God to fix things, I wised up. I shifted my point of view. I started seeing things through eyes of love. At least I *tried* to. I put my own little twist on it and changed my opinion of what was taking place above my head. I viewed the mother of the traveling tromping group as being sick. Perhaps this trip to the beach would be her last, and she was soon to die. Her children would weep bitterly and publicly. It would air on the ten o'clock news. It would show tearstained faces as they watch their mother's casket lowered into the red clay of Alabama. Maybe this vacation at the beach was to be for them one last moment in time together. This made me sad for the rug rats, those little bugger-chewers with clod feet. So I thought about their last trip to the beach. I pitied the sound above my head. It became something to endure as they moved and lived and enjoyed the last time with their mother. I even cleaned off the top of the broom handle and placed it back in the closet, never to be heard again.

When Your View Gets Flip-flopped

My change of tactics worked. No longer did I want God to burn them up with judgment. I even wanted a better view of them. I'd sized them up from a distance. Now I wanted a view that was close up and personal. If I were going to be sympathetic, I needed more info. So the next time I heard them descending the steps that led to the parking space below the condos, I watched. I went to the sliding glass door and stepped out onto the balcony, rubbernecking, trying to see beneath me. Then the strangest thing happened. One of the little girls dropped a cup. It rolled out into the byway between the condominiums, and I saw her. She was six—maybe. Not much older. She scooped up the cup and headed back beneath me. This is when I noticed why her steps were heavy above our heads. This is when I understood completely—she was pigeon-toed. To compound the difficulty of walking with a sideways kick of her feet, she had on flip-flops—pink ones with studded jewelry lining the straps. She probably bought them at Alvin's Island Tropical Department Store. And she was trying hard to keep them on her pigeon-toed feet. Smack. Smack. They slapped the pavement like a kid smacking the top of the ocean with a boogie board. Then, just as fast as she'd appeared, she disappeared beneath me. Maybe she was proud of those flip-flips. Maybe she slept in them the way I used to sleep in my cowboy boots when I was a kid. Maybe she walked so much above our heads because she liked the way they made her feel. Maybe those flip-flops changed everything for her. Maybe she was a princess or some kind of mermaid, riding the sea, kicking the ocean with the tips of her flip-flops. Maybe one day she will have those flip-flops on some shelf in her house as I have my cowboy boots on the bookcase in my study. Maybe they will mean as much to her. Maybe they will remind her of that first trip to the beach. Maybe her mom really *is* sick. It could be, you know. Who was I to mess things up? Her trip was priceless compared to my writing time. Maybe I don't know what spirit I'm of. None of us does. *Maybe this is our problem.*

WATCH OUT FOR THE ADDED LANE

What You Can't Add to Redemption's Power

MOST PEOPLE IN THE South know better than to use four-letter words at their minister's house. They can't say what they might say at home when they lock their keys in the car or drop something on the kitchen floor that splatters on the wall. In their homes, they can let four-letter words fly, such as *darn* or *dang*. And if they get real upset while watching their favorite football team lose, they might combine a four-letter word with a five-letter word, such as "shoot-fire." But when they come to the pastor's home, people with loose tongues know better. But there's the taboo word that doesn't fit the bill of being an offensive word. Most people overlook this word at social settings at my house. So Jill tips guests off.

"There's a certain word that should not be uttered under any circumstances," she tells our guests.

Guests are listening with rapt attention at this point, wondering if they've already used the word, replaying every word they've uttered from the door to the dining room table. Afraid they've said it. Afraid they have already hurt someone's feelings. And my wife cannot say the word either. She spells it.

"Bono, our boxer, must not hear the word W-A-L-K," she tells them. "Because when he hears it, he believes it is time for his W-A-L-K. And he gets revved up. He'll jump two feet off the ground and will continue to jump until I take him. So please don't say W-A-L-K."

Most guests nod their heads with empathy chiseled into their faces, as if to say, "Oh, yes, we know about that word. We would never use that word." But someone usually does. They slip up. They make a verbal misstep. Because life is a series of slipups and missteps.

A Misstep

One day Jill took Bono for a W-A-L-K that led to a misstep that probably led to a four-letter slipup. It happened on a clean, dimly lit path while I was tagging along with my little Jack Russell terrier named Spurgeon. We are dignified walkers, Spurgeon and I, so we usually trail behind the beauty and her beast. On this day around our neighborhood, we took a turn on the sidewalk that passes in front of one of the larger churches in town. It was a Sunday night, a busy night of Bible training. But we have no Sunday evening service at our church, and were tromping through their territory at high tide. A woman stopped my wife for a chat. Unbeknownst to her, some business took place behind her back. Bono figured he'd do some multitasking. Spurgeon and I spotted the tasking. We were embarrassed. We wanted to hold our noses and emit a "Pew!" like we knew nothing or no one. But Jill was clueless about the action behind her on the sidewalk; Spurgeon and I hurried past, pretending not to have noticed. When Jill joined us at the end of the block, I clued her in. She was shocked, looking down at Bono, who hung his head in shame. Then she dismissed the severity of the action. So I pleaded for three blocks, telling her how we had to make this right and clean up our mess.

"What if someone recognized me? They will trash my name in town. They'll go around telling everybody about what we left at the doorstep of one of the largest churches around. I can't have that."

Jill turned to face me as we walked up the front steps to our house.

The dogs were panting. The sky was a purple glaze. The sun was on its final descent. I stopped in front of her, and she said in a somber, matter-of-fact manner, "Robbie, you're not famous. No one recognized you."

She had a point. My church was barely a blip on the community's radar.

"But we can't just leave it there," I pleaded. "We have to go clean it up. It's the right thing to do."

She stood with her hands on her hips, sweat trickling into her neatly waxed eyebrows, and she conceded. "If it will make you feel better, we'll go do it."

"Feel better? It will make me feel like a pastor again."

We left Spurgeon behind; only the guilty one returned with us on a leash to the scene of the crime. Bono showed no remorse; neither did his owner—my wife. I was carrying the Wal-Mart plastic bags as we rounded the corner. People were coming and going out of the church's glass door; other parishioners congregated inside the huge plate-glass foyer. We watched them watching us. It was darker now. I crept up in a casual, nothing-wrong-here fashion. Just walking the dog. Then I went to a knee in a blinding flash, ready to scoop with a Wal-Mart bag in each hand, and just before I scooped, I saw. There was a tread mark in the middle. Maybe a tennis shoe or a fine pair of Cole Haan "Cedric Weave" loafers; I couldn't tell. It was dark. But someone had definitely made a misstep.

Maybe you have suffered a misstep. Maybe you married the wrong person, and now you suffer the consequences of a nasty divorce. Maybe you have committed a misstep by leaving one job for what you thought was a better one. Now you are having second thoughts. Missteps happen. The only thing I could do, kneeling on that tainted sidewalk, was to salvage what I could and leave the rest behind, because whoever made the misstep into the darkness never saw it coming. And life is a step here and a misstep there.

Sometimes we don't know how to move forward. This is the crossroads crisis.

Tread Lightly and Carry a Lamp

Crossroads are restless moments, a time of movement, where our feet have to go in some direction, even when we don't know where to step. This is where destiny meets the ordinary. It's what Buechner called "the hungering dark," a place where darkness hungers for great light. No one is prepared for the darkness we feel at a crossroads. Most of us take the well-lit path, the path that shines with promise. We believe the darkened way is not of God. But God never promised a clean, well-lit resort for our egos, only a lamp for our feet and a light for our path that leads out of this dark world (Ps. 119:105). We get confused because God leads only as we move. The lamp of the Old Testament didn't contain a halogen bulb. It was more like a weak flashlight. It illuminated only the steps immediately in front. Spurgeon said of the lamp in Psalm 119:105, "Having no fixed lamps in certain ancient towns, each person carried a lantern to avoid falling into the open sewer or stumbling over the heaps of manure that defiled the road. This is a true picture of our path through this dark world."[1] So we should take a watchful tiptoe in a direction around the manure of this place, knowing holy light will meet us and show us the next step. Because God's plan doesn't contain missteps. His timing is perfect. His light is efficient.

Travel Time

On vacations, we would bombard Dad with questions about time. "When are we going to get there?" "How much longer?"

Dad would never take the bait. He would shoot back, "We'll get there when we get there."

A small child cannot understand this type of reasoning. But it's the best possible one. Because my brother and I didn't have a clue about travel time. We just wanted to arrive. And for Dad to include us in his timetable meant he would have to explain what we weren't old enough to comprehend, such as miles per hour and distance. He could have answered, "We have 167 more miles to go, and we are traveling at sixty miles per hour. So do the math."

We didn't want to do the math. We wanted a straight answer. But he never gave one. Dad would not get involved in explaining time. It seems God doesn't either.

Time does not control God, and this is hard for us to comprehend and accept. We are dawdlers who lose blocks of time and accuse God of stealing them. We think he is slow. We wish he moved according to our schedule. But God will not get involved in time. He is above it. "But do not forget this one thing, dear friends: With the Lord a day is like a thousand years, and a thousand years are like a day. The Lord is not slow in keeping his promise, as some understand slowness" (2 Peter 3:8–9 NIV).

Our human ideas of lateness do not confine God. He sees all of history at once. What we deem as God's being late, he determines as the appointed time. So our attempts at involving God in time are about as futile as trying to get my dad to reveal his timetable. Dad had his appointed time, and we were supposed to enjoy the scenery without questioning travel time. My dad seemed to be saying, "Don't worry about tomorrow, for tomorrow will bring its own worries. Today's trouble is enough for today" (Matt. 6:34). But this is not good enough. We want to worry about tomorrow. We want tomorrow played out in Technicolor today. We want to know before we step. But sometimes all we get is Jesus' assurance that he has the travel time under control, and when we insert our own timetable, we bind ourselves to impatience and anxiety.

It is possible to get so tied up in our desires that we are unable to see the next step. We discover God's plan only as we remove our time constraints. William Barclay wrote, "There is comfort in the thought of a God who has all eternity to work in. It is only against the background of eternity that things appear in their true proportions and assume their real value."[2] Only when we place ourselves on eternal time do we attribute real value to life. We have time to work, not dawdle. Death is not the end of time. It is the end of time constraints but not our actual time. So much of our anxiety is birthed from a place of feeling that time is running out. "So be careful how you live, not as fools but as those who are wise. Make the most of every opportunity for doing good in these evil days. Don't act thoughtlessly, but try to understand what the Lord wants you to do" (Eph. 5:15–17). The King James Version reads, "Redeeming the time." And the step into the future is a redeeming step. But we allow time to trap us in the past, paralyzing the future.

Arthur Freeman and Rose DeWolf wrote in their book *Woulda Coulda, Shoulda,* "Remember that the way to cause bad memories to fade is to replace them with good memories, and the way to do that is to do something—to move ahead, to get involved in a project, to investigate possibilities."[3] We move forward as an agent of redemption—redeeming time. We make the most of our opportunities. Somewhere beyond our present crisis is a new beginning. But to see it, we must reinterpret the way we view ourselves in relation to time.

And change happens as we clean out some old ways of thinking. "Don't copy the behavior and customs of this world, but let God transform you into a new person by changing the way you think" (Rom. 12:2). Some fixed beliefs have to go, such as "I'm broken beyond repair." To free ourselves, we must redeem this entrenched thought. Like Noah, we can't reinterpret the future by fixating on the destruction left by our crisis. Noah did not have topographical maps to go by. It was a new world. He had to let go of the past. Stop mourning the days before the flood. Life was predictable then. But he had to step out of the ark and make his way in the new world. We do too. Our setbacks are only temporary. And redemption is a process, not an event. I discovered this in a pair of trees a friend found in a Wal-Mart dumpster.

Redemption in a Wal-Mart Dumpster

The lesson came by way of the green thumb of Lucille, which would make Martha Stewart envious. She's a tree's best friend, especially one discarded in Wal-Mart's dumpster. She digs these left-for-dead trees out and breathes new life into them.

I witnessed it on a Saturday. Jill and I still lived in the basement of her parents' house, and I was helping her father do yard work. It was humid. The dog days of summer lounged at the corners of clouds wilted by a deepening sunset. When the gravel of the driveway crackled beneath the weight of Lucille's white Cadillac, we looked up from our work. The Cadillac had sticks hanging from the trunk—poor sticks, needle-thin sticks. But she told my father-in-law that if he allowed her to plant these "trees" in his backyard, she'd resurrect them. She would personally make sure they thrived. I was thinking, *This woman is nuts. These sticks won't live. Wal-Mart gave up on them.* When Wal-Mart gives up, it means serious decay!

I kept my mouth shut while my father-in-law took those sticks and planted two of them in his backyard. When Lucille came over to our basement for a weekly Bible study, she watered them, fertilized them, and bathed them with love. Every morning, as the summer progressed into fall, I'd look out the kitchen window at those sticks propped up and staked with twine. I'd shake my head and laugh at the absurdity of it all. Lucille was delusional. What looked like a stick yesterday looked like a stick today. But Lucille wasn't discouraged. She kept nurturing and believing that what was once dead could live again. While I judged their appearance, she clung to her faith in the invisible power of redemption.

One morning, while making coffee, I glanced out the window and noticed there were leaves on those sticks. Hope springs eternal! Literally. There were more leaves the next day. And in the grasp of fall's seasonal change, the hills of Tennessee caught fire as the leaves of the trees burned fluorescent orange. And the Wal-Mart rejects stood in upright determination, blazing with holy change.

At one time, the trees faced death in a Wal-Mart Dumpster. But in the hands of Lucille, resurrection happened. So it is with our souls. Becoming more like Christ is a process, not an event. Flannery O'Connor once said, "There is something in us, as storytellers and as listeners to stories, that demands the redemptive act, that demands that what falls at least be offered the chance to be restored."[4] This is good theology. Lucille theology. In the light of eternity, the redemptive act has time to work.

All of us can start somewhere in the process of redemption. We can redeem the time we waste watching television or searching the Internet at random. We can make the most of our opportunities by finding comfort in the thought that God has all of eternity to perform his work. When redemption is hidden by present brokenness, it doesn't mean it is not working. Ask Lucille. Ask William Barclay. He said, "It is only against the background of eternity that things appear in their true proportions and assume their real value."[5] So ask, "Will what I'm worrying about mean anything in eternity?" This is how we use time as a step into the future. We focus only on what will have eternal value. We calibrate our lives according to eternal time. It's living by making the most out of our opportunities—redeeming time. Death is not the end. Missteps will not permanently affect us. They are only temporary setbacks in the light of eternity. But we have the tendency to let our lives drift when we encounter failure. And Frederick Buechner believes that we are in constant danger of being not actors in the drama of our lives but reactors. He wrote, "When good things happen, we rise to heaven; when bad things happen, we descend to hell."[6] This is life according to which way the wind blows. It's not a life of steady redemption.

What We Learn from Noah's Voyage

When we say, "This happened; now I'm eternally broken," or "They did this; now they can never be forgiven," we forget God redeems. This is his focus in our fallen world. And redemption takes time. There is no hurry in the heart of God. "God waited patiently while Noah was build-ing his boat" (1 Peter 3:20). God could have snapped his fingers and created an ark. He wasn't short on creative juice. He was long on patience. I'm sure Noah and God both had their moments. Boards were too short. The consistency of the pitch failed inspection. God could have fired slowpoke Noah and given him a pink slip, along with direc-tions to the unemployment office. God had enough influence to hire a team of engineers. He could have imported the finest pitch known to man. Could have rained down nails and hung power saws in trees. But God was patient with Noah. He offered a time span of 120 years. Wherever we find redemption, we find God's patience. But to see it, we must reinterpret the way we view time.

The flood caused Noah to rethink his future. For 120 years, Noah's life revolved around making the ark, then sailing the tub. He had grown accustomed to the swing of the hammer. Then the rain raised the water and the ark floated. Then the rain stopped and the water receded. And Noah stepped out into a new world. His eyes needed time to adjust to the sun. He'd just witnessed a flood. Mankind had drowned in his own bathtub. There was evidence of death all around. Yesterday tainted the new day, as the earth flapped like a sheet on a Midwest clothesline. It must have been strange for Noah, but out of this period of uncertainty, a new beginning emerged. Trees blossomed. Grass stood tall. Turtles climbed from the ark with gothic motions. Birds rediscovered the branch of a tree. They perched and looked around in horror at the dev-astation of the flood.

Maybe you've had the same look of horror. You've been through a devastating divorce. You've made a misstep into the darkness. Now you are on the other side of it. The landscape looks bleak. Maybe you let someone down. You hurt a friend. You walked away at a critical time. Or perhaps something went terribly wrong. Now you have only the devastation and the faint hope of a new beginning.

To get a new beginning, we have to get a new lay of the land. It's a world of new thoughts and feelings and beliefs. Things don't change overnight. We have to step away from the old life. "... throw off your old evil nature and your former way of life, which is rotten through and through, full of lust and deception. Instead, there must be a spiritual renewal of your thoughts and attitudes" (Eph. 4:22–23). This is no easy task, so we find ourselves reverting to things that offer temporary relief, such as alcohol, drugs, binge eating, Internet porn, and so forth.

The one thing to remember in light of eternity is that failure is not permanent, only a temporary setback. The way we interpret our missteps predicts what we do with the future. Those who see a failure as a temporary setback operate outside of time. They understand eternity starts now. We need only to begin a new journey. And maybe you have made a series of missteps. Now you are hidden in darkness and confusion. The way out is to take a step of faith. Put the past behind you. Learn what it means to forget. The apostle Paul wrote, "No, dear brothers and sisters, I am still not all I should be, but I am focusing all my energies on this one thing: Forgetting the past and looking forward to what lies ahead, I strain to reach the end of the race and receive the prize for which God, through Christ Jesus, is calling us up to heaven" (Phil. 3:13–14). Past performance keeps us from taking a step of faith. We fear failure may happen again. Yet we should move beyond it.

The Giant Step Forward

There's a Chinese saying: "A journey of a thousand miles begins with a single step." Light illumines our path one step at a time when we choose to travel blind like Abraham, not knowing exactly where we are going or how long it will take to arrive. But moving nonetheless toward what looks like darkness, knowing holy light will somehow meet us there. God leads as we move. And as Frederick Buechner said, "None of us know much about where we are going really, not in the long run anyway, beyond the next mountain. We keep busy. We climb. We learn. We grow. Hopefully. But we are going, I believe, much, much further than at this point we can possibly see, and in everything we do or fail to do, much more is at stake, I believe, than we dream. In this life and in whatever life awaits us, he is the way; that is our faith."[7]

When we submit to God's timetable through prayer, we relinquish our travel plans and move beyond the time constraints of this world. We take a step of faith, knowing "underneath are the everlasting arms" (Deut. 33:27 NIV).

THE BUMP IN EVERY ROAD

What You Should Watch Out For

WHEN I MARRIED JILL, I wasn't truthful. I wasn't completely honest. I didn't tell her about one of my flaws, the one that looks like a claw on the foot of Godzilla.

I can remember the day she spotted it.

"What's wrong with your toe?"

"You mean this thing?"

Busted.

Maybe I should have sat her down and said, "Listen, I've got this claw that looks like some kind of weird lizard gene, but it's really a toe ... I promise." I should have told her, because when the honeymoon is over, we usually start showing our true colors. I could no longer hide the claw.

Not only did it look horrendous, but it could wound as well. She didn't know that I flopped like a fish in the bed, and if I flopped a certain way, the claw could take a hunk of leg on the way down. The claw became one of Jill's greatest nightmares. It hunted her down in the night. It jabbed and poked her. It tore the sheets. Finally she started jostling me in bed, saying, "You got me with that claw."

She never counted on the claw when she said, "I do."

"Do you, Jill Whitehurst, take this claw to love and to hold, from this gouge forward?"

She never saw the claw coming. I believed that exposing my hidden parts would make me unlovable. No matter what we desire, the last thing we want is to be unloved. We will go to extremes to feel loved. So I hid the claw. There was no remedy.

The curse of the claw has jabbed us all. The gene of dysfunction is in us. Adam has passed it down. My human claw is like the sinful nature found inside each of us. "... because of my sinful nature I am a slave to sin" (Rom. 7:25). It's what we call "original sin."

The church has given up a lot of ground in this area. We've handed the lamp to psychologists, who, like mechanics with flashlights, have examined the human claw. Jung named it the *shadow self*. And when Jill says something about the claw, I respond, "That's not a toe. That's the shadow self."

"I don't care what you call it. Get it off me. Keep it on your side of the bed."

So we have tried to get free from the human claw. But psychology has proven unable to cure it; all psychology has accomplished is to analyze and rename it. Psychologist Robert Ewen describes our "claw" as "the primitive and unwelcome side of personality that derives from our animal forbears."[1]

Jung concurs with Christianity; the goal is to curtail the human claw's growth. As Jill would say, "Clip the claw. Get a pedicure. Reduce the size of that thing."

Reducing the claw's size would be a good thing. But it doesn't stop the claw. It still likes to gouge and injure. It's incorrigible, this claw of mine.

Is it an animal? Not really. The human claw is my fallen nature that is at war with my spirit. It is an inner moral conflict (Rom. 7:18). Left to myself, the claw wins. It grows until it becomes evil in all its ways. This is why Jung had a hard time with fallen human nature. Renaming evil does not eradicate it. Something more powerful must engage and overcome its tendencies. This is why Christ paid the price on Calvary, to defeat sin. Otherwise, it's like Jesus' parable of the empty house (Matt. 12:43). George Buttrick, in his commentary *The Parables of Jesus,* stated, "To drive out false masters from the soul and leave the house of personality unoccupied might be a policy of disaster ... overcome with disappointment over our failure in reform, we deliver the house to the abandon of despair—and our last state becomes worse than the first."[2]

The only hope in defeating the sinful nature is to live by the Spirit. Then "you will not gratify the desires of the sinful nature" (Gal. 5:16 NIV).

Jung instructed us to *embrace* our shadow selves. He believed that, instead of "turning away in disgust from our shadow, we must open this Pandora's Box and accept its contents."[3] The word *accept* is where Jung led us astray.

The goal, as C. S. Lewis and evangelicals identify it, is not to become an authentic *individualized self* but to become authentically *Christlike.* The objective is to build up what Lewis called the "central part of you." He is referring to the part of you that makes up your "life as a whole, with all your innumerable choices, all your life long you are slowly turning this central thing either into a heavenly creature or into a hellish creature...."[4]

Self-discovery is not bad. It's essential. We should bring hidden sin and habits into the light (Mark 4:22). Then we are responsible for revealed sin. What we do with what we find in Pandora's box makes all the difference. We don't embrace it. We subject it to Christ's forgiveness and spiritual formation.

On the Heels of Sainthood

Accepting Christ doesn't eradicate our fallen human nature. As new Christians, we still have to struggle with the results of past sin. We still reap what we've sown. It takes awhile to reap the good things we begin to sow at the moment of salvation. "So don't get tired of doing what is good. Don't get discouraged and give up, for we will reap a harvest of blessing at the appropriate time" (Gal. 6:9).

Spiritual formation is, at least in part, the making of right moral choices. Of course, it doesn't mean just *acting* moral. The Pharisees spelled the doom of that tradition. C. S. Lewis said morality has to do with three choices. "Firstly, with fair play and harmony between individuals. Secondly, with what might be called tidying up or harmonizing the things inside each individual. Thirdly, with the general purpose of human life as a whole: what man was made for."[5] This is a broad overview of spiritual formation. The first choice is plain and global. The second is the inner conflicts. The third choice includes the worship of God. It's learning how to become more Christlike.

Spiritual formation is not synonymous with salvation; it's not that we have a license to sin. Neither does it consist of working our way to heaven. Spiritual formation is, instead, a process whereby we work to bring our "hidden things" into Christ's light.

Working from a Place of Safety

Everyone needs to enter the process of spiritual formation, which results in genuine Christlikeness. We should go easier on *ourselves* while getting tough with *sin*. We must find a place of peace to work from while attacking sin during the growth process. Jeremiah wrote, "... we bear your name; do not forsake us" (Jer. 14:9). This is the place of safety. Before we can work on eradicating sin, we must settle the issue of whom we belong to—God or Satan. If we belong to God, then we bear his name, and he will not forsake us. "And I am convinced that nothing can ever separate us from his love. Death can't, and life can't. The angels can't, and the demons can't. Our fears for today, our worries about tomorrow, and even the powers of hell can't keep God's love away" (Rom. 8:38). We need to keep this assurance.

When we get off track, God's love hasn't abandoned us. It is still growing. So when you sin—and you *will* sin—don't ever doubt the ownership of your soul. Satan wants you to believe when you've committed a sin that he owns you again. He does not. It would be like Noah having a hole in the ark, and instead of fixing it, abandoning ship to the flood. Maybe Noah had a few leaks in the ark. Perhaps he carried aboard some extra pitch. Maybe the first ten days the ark leaked like a sieve. But he stayed his course. Noah trusted God for the outcome. We are, in a sense, in the ark of Christ, closed off from outside destruction. We will eventually reach solid ground in our new world. The flood of sin will be over. In the meantime, however, we voyage on the sea of a fallen world, with waves of sin slapping the hull, as we await death's final defeat. We may spring a leak, but we never abandon ship. We begin to turn old emotions and thoughts into new ones. "... throw off your old evil nature and your former way of life, which is rotten through and through, full of lust and deception. Instead, there must be a spiritual renewal of your thoughts and attitudes" (Eph. 4:22–23).

An all-important truth to embrace is that the means of change determines the end result. I discovered this on a plane trip to Brisbane, Australia.

The Means Determines the End

He stumbled into the waiting area with a lit cigarette and a beer. He scanned the room and selected the seat next to me. I was on my way to Brisbane, Australia, to speak at a youth conference. I had an hour layover in Los Angeles. The guy positioned himself to occupy my time. He was elated the Cleveland Indians were on their way to the World Series. He'd periodically take off his hat and speak to the Indians mascot. Then he'd give a cheer with a few choice words. Thirty minutes into the pep rally, he switched gears and talked about his trip to Australia. He was going to meet his brother in Sydney and become a student of underwater welding. He described the whole method: how they dove, how they welded, and how they'd go out to drink after work. He said it with gusto. I knew I was facing an eighteen-hour, nonstop flight from Los Angeles to Sydney with this guy.

Toward the end of the layover, I was thinking, *God, how much longer will I have to endure this guy?* Then things turned my way. He took a swig of his beer and said, "Why are you going to Australia?"

Oh, how sweet it is when life turns your way! I'd been waiting for this moment. It was my turn! "I'm going over to save souls, especially those from Cleveland."

No, actually, I let him off a little easier than that. I said, "I'm going over to speak to teenagers. I'm a pastor."

Saved by a call to board the plane, the drunken Indians fan stuck his cigarette between his lips and poked his hand through the smoke for a good shake. He said, "Good luck" out of the side of his mouth that wasn't holding the cigarette.

We both prayed we wouldn't have to sit near each other. I stalled by searching my computer bag. I gave him room to make his getaway. I was thinking that God must have an enormous amount of patience. If I were God, I'd set this guy's breath on fire. He would become an all-consuming fire. Then crumble to ashes. But God is more mature. "He does not want anyone to perish, so he is giving more time for everyone to repent" (2 Peter 3:9).

Sleeping Like a Baby on Liquid Tylenol

As we boarded the plane, I kept my eye on the Indians fan. Thank God, he was ten rows up and on the opposite side of the jumbo jet. I watched him ask the stewardess for a pillow. Then he pulled his Indians hat over his eyes and slept like a baby on liquid Tylenol. I watched him for eighteen hours while I thrashed around on my side of the plane. For eighteen hours he never moved his head. He slept the whole way. I wanted to go over and give him a wet-willie or a noogie. Ruffle his sleep. Shout "GO INDIANS!" in his ear and take his hat off and stomp it in the aisle. Anything to wake him.

Then I realized that this drunken fan had a method to his madness. Someone had tipped him off. Maybe his brother called him up and said, "Now, listen. This is what you need to do. The night before your flight, stay up. Don't sleep. Then before leaving for the airport, take some Tylenol PM. After checking your bags, go to the bar. Get hammered. Drink until the call to board the plane is made, and you'll sleep like a baby the entire trip."

I'm not condoning such a method, but if his brother actually tipped him off, then the Indians fan had followed the method to a tee. And it worked! He traveled to Sydney like a duffel bag, while I struggled in my seat through the eighteenth hour.

We tend to believe the means to redemption should never over-shadow our goal of happiness and success, because selfish pursuit demands happiness on our terms. The means of spiritual formation is not pain-free. We will suffer and cry during our development. Harry Emerson Fosdick noted, the "trouble is that when it comes to genuine Christian living, fine in quality, radiant in influence, steady in difficulty, victorious in temptation, aware of inward resources of spiritual power, we applaud the ideal but we take no pains with the means of reaching it."[6]

We invite Christ to infuse us with his patience by "constant prac-ticed methods—worship, prayer, quiet hours, directed reading, directed meditation, fellowship in the church, where the social forces of com-mon aspiration come to our help."[7] We continually admit weakness so we can grasp his strength. This may at times make us unhappy. God's patience is the means that determines the end. Harry Emerson Fosdick wrote, "... our wills cannot deal directly with ends, only with means, so that, making idealistic decisions about ends and letting the means take care of themselves, we wake up to discover that the means have determined the ends."[8]

When we submit our wills to God's patience, we allow God to

determine the means of spiritual formation. Saint Augustine instructed us to "Pray as though everything depended on God. Work as though everything depended on you." It makes sense. When we submit to God's timetable through prayer, we release the ends. We work on the means. The means is prayer and submission. Use a different means and we will never undergo spiritual transformation. Just ask my fellow traveler to Brisbane, Australia. He had a method to his madness. He started with a means to reach an idealistic end. He wanted to sleep the eighteen hours away. But the end he discovered was surely different from the one he envisioned.

And at first, I thought, *That's not fair. I struggled. Stayed awake and felt the pain of travel.* Then when our flight ended, I watched him lumber from the plane. He walked like a dead man in a snowstorm wearing oversized galoshes, not like a man who'd taken an eighteen-hour nap. Each step through the gate was a laborious muddling. According to C. S. Lewis, a means that results in good fortune in the short run may be a dangerous thing in the long run.[9] This man suffered the consequences of his actions.

My Indians fan may have slept, but he missed out. He missed the beauty of the sky at dusk—a soft violet over puffy melon clouds—the mystery of the light behind, splashing through the plane's window. He missed the journey. He had no idea of how a warm cloth felt on the back of a neck in the sixteenth hour. He will never know the peace I found reading my Bible, studying grace, and how it filled me with praise. Nor will he ever know how I prayed when the plane hopped clouds and landed on its belly, terrified that my hour had come, the same way Buechner felt while riding a plane. In Buechner's moment he remembered a line from Deuteronomy: "underneath are the everlasting arms." He said that for a few minutes he understood and felt in his "nethermost depths" that it was true, that God was "underneath, under girding, transcending any disaster that could possibly happen," that God's arms would be there to save him if the plane fell from the sky. And in that tumultuous plane, miles from the earth, he was not afraid. He wrote, "I found myself not only not afraid of what was going on, but enormously enjoying it, half drunk on the knowledge that yes, it was true. There was nothing to worry about. There was no reason to fear. It was all of it, *all* of it, and forever and always good."[10]

Looking back, I can see it written all over the Indians fan's face. There was a strategy to his madness. But his means determined his end. It cost him. He would never know a moment like Buechner's moment of faith, which was so much like my moment of assurance. "Look to the road you are walking on! He who picks up one end of a stick picks up the other," wrote Fosdick. "He who chooses the beginning of a road chooses the place it leads to. It is the means that determine the end."[11]

THE LIFE YOU SAVE MAY BE YOUR OWN

Taking Control of Dangerous Emotions

IT STARTED WITH SCRATCHING noises and ended in tragedy.

"Dad, there's something in my room. It sounds like a small dog running across the ceiling," Blair said.

"Nonsense. Go back to bed."

"Dad, get up!"

"Whatever it is, it can't get in," I said, pulling the covers up to my chin, not wanting to leave my warm cocoon.

"Dad! It's scratching and keeping me up. Please do something!"

"Okay, hang on."

"Hurry!"

She was right. It sounded like a party between the floors. The next morning I called a pest control company about the late-night noise. They sent over some sticky-boards for mice that included directions to put bait in the middle and leave it out for the critters. I followed the directions.

The next morning, the cheese was gone, but there was no mouse. I tried again, same thing—no cheese and no mouse. I called the pest control guy and described my dilemma.

"I'll be right over."

The dust flew up when he hit the driveway. The brakes squealed. The door flew open. He held up one finger. I waited. He lifted the rear deck on his truck and pulled out the mother lode of all sticky-boards. It could've doubled for a window shade for the windshield of his truck. He was grinning. I was grinning. He repositioned the Skoal tucked in his lip and said, "This right here, Mr. Stofel, will catch a snake if it was to crawl up here on it. Watch." He stuck his finger in the center and stretched the sticky stuff away from the board. "Guaranteed," he said.

"What do I do if I catch one?"

"Kill it."

"Kill it?"

"Yep."

"How?"

"Pert'near anything you hit him with ought to kill him."

"Okay." I was innocent.

That night, I huddled the family. "This is the bazooka. The party is over. He's mine!"

They watched as I placed it on the kitchen floor. Then I turned to face them and said, "Now let's see who does some scratching tonight."

"You're getting into this mouse thing, aren't you, Dad?"

I grinned and broke the huddle.

Coming Unglued

About 4:00 a.m. Spurgeon started barking. I got up and eased to the edge of the kitchen, approaching the closed door. It sounded like a fish flopping in the bottom of an aluminum boat. I crept closer and placed my ear to the crack of the door. My heart dropped. I knew what to do next. I woke my wife. She came to where I was listening. "Do you hear that?" I said. "He's got to be huge." The animal was growing in my imagination with every flop.

She said, "Go in there and see what's on the board."

"I'm not going in there." As far as I was concerned, the game had changed. I thought I was hunting down Mickey Mouse, not Super Rat.

"Get in there and take care of it. That's why I married you."

I rolled my eyes.

We listened and it flopped. Then there was a long stretch of silence.

"Maybe it's dead," Jill said. "Go on in there and get it, you big sissy."

What's a man to do? I eased my way into the kitchen, and when it saw me, it did a somersault. I slammed the door and turned to Jill. "It's huge."

"Go get a box to put over it," she calmly directed. "Then scoop it into the box."

"Are you crazy?"

"You got a better idea?"

I got a shovel from the garage. I wasn't about to put my hand at eye-level with that monster. I figured I could scoop him up, board and all, and place him in the trash container. It would be a slow death, but—

The snow shovel bounced and scraped across the tiled floor. I was standing on a kitchen chair. He was a big boy! When I tried to scoop him up, I accidentally knocked his front feet off the sticky-board. He began scratching, trying to get off. That pest control man was right. The sticky-board had trapped my shovel. It wouldn't budge. There I stood on a kitchen chair with a shovel stuck on the pest control board, with a river rat that had made its way three blocks from the Tennessee River to my kitchen. I was afraid to move, afraid I'd knock the other two feet off. Then I'd have a live rat chasing me. So I began screaming, "Jill, go get another shovel!"

Five minutes later—she couldn't find the shovel—she was back to the edge of the kitchen.

"Where'd you go? Wal-Mart?"

She smirked and stretched the shovel into my extended hand. She had finally found it. I grabbed it and tried my best to hold on to the one shovel, while repositioning the other with one hand so I could get a better grip. Then Jill joined my daughter, who was standing on the church pew in the hall. They were screaming. So was the rat.

I thought how the homicide might go down. I remembered playing the board game Clue. I remembered the blunt objects of the game, and I knew what to do. I swung the shovel and missed—steel against tile. Swung again. Missed again. Then the third attempt connected. It ended the screaming and the scratching. The kitchen became a gruesome homicide scene.

To this day, that rat still screams and digs into some far recess of my brain. Even now, when I go to the kitchen, I can see the whole ordeal, the struggle, the sound, the way it died. It left a lasting impression.

Memories of past tragedies can haunt us. They make hostages of our emotions and tell us that what we feel is real. It can be confusing. Which is real? The emotions we feel about the facts or the facts themselves? Most of the time, our emotions win. Dennis Morgan believes "emotions dictate the interpretation of every piece of information.... How we feel becomes more real than truth."[1] After a divorce, we often assume everyone else will reject us. We say to ourselves, *Why bother? Why try again? There's no one out there for me. Broken beyond repair. Besides, I'll just get hurt again.*

This is how we often interpret our emotions. And those emotions can shape our future. We believe a lie and then proceed to shape our lives around that lie. It happened to me when I was twelve.

Forefathers' Revenge

The year I turned twelve, I was accosted walking home from school. It was a pivotal moment, a moment when my worldview changed.

African-Americans lived in the neighborhood across Carter's Creek Pike in front of Jewell's Market. We lived a block behind the market, and

African-Americans would walk through our neighborhood to school. In the segregated South, they walked on one side of the road and we walked on the other. We lived in our own separate worlds until those worlds collided.

My shortcut home was to jump the milky creek and cut through the wooded area in front of my house. It saved walking an extra block to the bridge. I'd cut enough time off the walk to catch the beginning of *Gilligan's Island*. I walked alone that day. My brother was home sick. When I jumped across to the other side, my red Converse tennis shoes slipped, and for a second I went down to one knee. Before I could get up, Reggie jumped me from behind, took me to the ground, sat on top of me, and beat my face with his fists while saying, "This is for my forefathers. You should've known better than mess with us. We're not slaves!"

Finally, one of Reggie's friends told him to come on or they were going to leave without him. I guess it was shameful to watch a boy getting beat up without slinging the first fist. Reggie had jumped me so quickly and stunned me so badly with his words that he had immobilized me. He took one last swing, biting the bottom of his lip in concentration, and then ran to catch up with his friends. I watched the red mud fall from his shoes as he stepped away.

I had no idea why he beat me up. I couldn't understand what the color of my skin and my southern roots had to do with slavery. I didn't know anything about slavery. I started asking myself some hard questions. Was I guilty? Do all African-Americans feel the same as Reggie? I start imagining every black man hated me.

I carried that racial baggage for twenty-five years, feeling uncomfortable in the presence of any African-American. Unable to look them in the eyes. I felt guilty, even though I'd never lifted a finger to hurt them. I didn't hate them, but I lived a long time with false guilt.

It's hard to let go of false emotions. They become real over an extended period. We believe their lies. We are greyhounds at the dog track. The gate opens, the rabbit runs, and so do the greyhounds. It is all they know.

It is the same with us. The gate of our emotions opens, and we run with damaged thoughts. Sometimes all we know is sadness. It wakes us and runs us. It interprets what we see. We know something is not quite right about what we feel, but we can't stop the pain. Psychologists call it "emotional reasoning." Our thinking is affected by how we feel. According to Freeman and DeWolf, to reverse emotional reasoning, we have to change the emotions we feel.[2] Old thoughts have to change (Rom. 12:2).

Ernest Ligon believes the way to stop our emotions from governing our thinking is to pray a particular portion of the Lord's Prayer. "May your will be done here on earth, just as it is in heaven" (Matt. 6:10). He believes this is a spiritual principle practiced in heaven. And since God's will directs our lives, this is a principle by which we must operate. In the midst of a crisis we need to subject every thought to the following questions: How would heaven respond to my situation? How would I act if I were experiencing this crisis in heaven? We can learn to think in heavenly terms.

We snare ourselves by concluding that God agrees with our emotional reasoning. Emotional reasoning warps our faith and makes excuses for our behavior. It ultimately leads to the false belief that our relationship with God is based on feelings: I feel joy, so my behavior must be in God's will, even though it may involve an illicit affair. Thus we fall into the trap of erroneous belief that God wants us to be happy more than he wants us to be holy.

God's will is known by reading God's Word and by the Spirit, which doesn't negate all emotion. But the Spirit never guides us based on all feelings. "But when he, the Spirit of truth, comes, he will guide you into all truth" (John 16:13 NIV). So when the Spirit guides us, it will be in truth. We cannot lie and make excuses if the Spirit leads us. We have to be honest with our emotions. We have to hit false emotions with the blunt truth. The only way they are going to get off the sticky-board of our hearts is to kill them with truth.

I could have blamed the pest control man. I could have called and told him how crazy he was for giving me the sticky-board in the first place. But I agreed to take it. I placed it on the floor. I killed the rodent.

As a result of my run-in with Reggie near Carter's Creek Pike, I subjected myself to false emotions for over twenty years. I erroneously believed that every African-American hated me.

The Illusion Is the Delusion

After finishing a degree in psychology, I took a job at a halfway house for crack addicts in the inner city of Nashville, where I led Bible studies and offered biblical counseling to a predominantly African-American population. It became increasing evident that God was working on me as much as he was working on those fellows. I realized that, somewhere deep inside me, I was sick and hiding from the pain. I didn't understand the depth of my demons stemming from the milky creek beating. Every time I was around one of those men, I felt fear. I didn't trust them. I imagined they hated me. Finally one Tuesday in a group session, my emotions tumbled out into the open. It happened during a little exercise of trust.

Counselor, Heal Thyself

"Okay, today we're going to take a trust test," I said after I'd gathered the group in the activity room.

"We're doing what?" asked Leon, who had revealed the week before that he was illiterate.

"Leon, help me move this table into the middle of the room." I gripped the edge of a rickety table that sat in the corner. "Everybody has to climb this table and fall backward into the arms of your group." We centered it in the room and Leon, now realizing that it wasn't a written test, was smiling with enthusiasm.

I said, "Form two lines at this end and cradle your arms out in front of you. You're going to catch Joseph."

They laughed and rushed to form two lines.

"You ain't catching me!" Joseph protested. "Huh-uh. No, sir, not me."

"What? Are you scared?" I knew a little mob psychology would work.

"Yeah, what you afraid of?" They all began to chime in. "You big sissy. Climb on up there. We'll catch your skinny butt."

I instructed Joseph to stand on the table. He wagged his head and climbed up.

"I want you to put the back of your heels at the edge of the table, cross your arms in front, and close your eyes."

Joseph positioned himself.

"Now. When I yell, 'Ready, team?' I want the catchers on the floor to yell back, 'Ready!' That way I know everybody's on the same team."

I looked at the poor trembling soul on the table and asked if he was ready.

"I'm telling you, you better not drop me," he begged, as he looked behind him at the eleven recovering crack addicts, not sure their hands would be there to catch him. The men jerked their hands away, hiding them behind their backs.

They all laughed, and Tommy said, "You just worry about falling, and we'll do the catching. Let's go."

"Okay. Ready, team?"

"Ready!" they shouted in unison.

"Okay, Joseph, fall!"

In a cumbersome straight-board fashion Joseph fell back. Then he buckled his knees and tried to assist in breaking the fall. When he did, they all hissed, "What was that?"

They made him climb back up and fall again until he became a trapeze artist. Each of the others followed, and when each success-fully completed his fall, the catchers would shout, "All right! Way to go!"

Each mastered his fear. Each trusted the other person. What a process of change! They got quiet and pointed at me. "It's your turn."

"My turn? No, you don't understand the rules. The counselor never becomes the counselee. He doesn't take the fall. He oversees it." Why was I hesitant to climb the table and fall? Was I afraid of falling into the hands of recovering crack addicts? Or was I afraid to fall into the hands of these men?

"No," they said, "you don't understand. You're climbing the table."

"The exercise is over. Go back to your seats."

But they inched closer to me as if they were going to grab me and stand me on the table. It frightened me for a second to see these guys coming toward me. It was my moment of decision. Were the feelings I felt in that moment false or real? Were they coming at me like Reggie had? I looked at that rickety table. I looked at them. I contemplated my rights as a counselor, rights to deny the request, to keep the power, but I knew what I had to do. I climbed the table and looked back at twelve homeless crack addicts.

As they got into position, I waited for the command. It came to me in a surreal voice, "Okay, fall!" I took the plunge, landing on a cushion of black hands. At that moment, I was free, unshackled. I lay there looking up into their laughing faces that just the week before I had taken to see John Grisham's *A Time to Kill*. I sat next to them in that dark theater listening to the men groan as the little black girl was abused by the two rednecks and then left for dead. Now I lay in their arms looking, for a brief moment, into faces I was scared to look at while the movie flickered. At the end of the movie, when the white lawyer went to the African-American man's house for a picnic and to let their children play together, I wanted to be that white man. I wanted to step into the scene and feel acceptance and mutual love. For the first time, I didn't feel those old emotions from the milky creek incident. They were false! I felt accepted. The fall was a rite of passage back to civilization.

They stood me on my feet and laughed, hugging me, and patting me on the back. They didn't have a clue. I never told them what was going on inside.

For three years I faithfully ministered to them. I even took the healing to the next level and invited ten of them over to my house to watch a boxing match on Pay-Per-View. We grilled steaks, gathered around the television, and watched boxing. They yelled and whooped it up. I was healed.

They never sensed the healing that took place inside me. I realized the emotions I had lived with all those years were false. The wounded healer was healed.

Maybe you are dealing with some damaged emotions. Check to see if they are real. Then ruthlessly eliminate the false. It makes us whole. It drives away our "rat thinking." I guarantee you; I'll never use another sticky-board to catch a rat. There's no way I'm going to kill another one. When we think of emotional pain in rat terms, the truth will always steer us clear of sin, because whatever is trapped on the sticky-board must be killed.

THE NORTHERNMOST HANG-UP

How to Change Direction Midstream

I CRUSHED MY FINGER and pulled a back muscle the winter it snowed 121 inches in the Boston area. It seemed the sky dropped snowflakes the size of boulders. I attended seminary during the day and worked the graveyard shift at UPS. It was a job—a means to an end. I carpooled with Bruce and David. Bruce lived across the hall in married housing. We'd meet in the parking lot around ten and tuck ourselves into a long night of lifting boxes, stacking them, and rearranging them when they fell. Some heavy. Others deceptively light. We were theologians in the rough. We needed a job—UPS paid part of our tuition. The paycheck helped me move my family from Tennessee to the Gordon-Conwell Theological Seminary in South Hamilton, Massachusetts. Jill and I decided I should move there first. She'd live with my mother in Tennessee for the first semester. She'd join me after I settled into a job. Then God moved in the depths of 121 inches of snow and in signs that could only be viewed as miraculous.

Wrong Zip Codes

The first few weeks of work at UPS, they assign a trainer who leans against the trailer of the semi and shouts, "Bend your knees. I want your *legs* to hurt, not your *back*." When we got it right, he'd say, "That's it." Then he'd try to slip a box with the wrong zip code onto our conveyer belt when we weren't looking. We had to remember a good six zip codes, and if we missed his "planted" box and stacked it with the rest of the ones going north to Bangor, Maine, he'd bust us. This place would be my "northernmost hang-up," as Jack Kerouac called his flubbed attempt to go westward by first going north. Let me explain.

The Northernmost Hang-up

At the beginning of Jack Kerouac's novel *On the Road* (1955), Sal Paradise has dreams of going westward from New York. So he pores over maps and makes his decision to go west by traveling Route 6. That pike is one long red line that stretched "from the tip of Cape Cod clear to Ely, Nevada, and there dipped down to Los Angeles."[1] Chicago was the first goal on his trip, so he heads out of New York toward Bear Mountain, making his way northward to join Route 6. But he soon discovers that Route 6 over Bear Mountain is a poor decision. "I was forty miles north of New York; all the way up I'd been worried about the fact that on this, my big opening day, I was only moving north instead of the so-longed-for west. Now I was stuck on my northernmost hang-up."[2] His California dream stalls. And after Sal hitched a ride, the man behind the wheel tells Sal, "... no traffic passes through 6. If you want to go to Chicago you'd do better going across the Holland Tunnel in New York and head for Pittsburgh." And Sal says, "... I knew he was right. It was my dream that screwed up, the stupid hearthside idea that it would be wonderful to follow one great red line across America instead of trying various roads...."[3]

Like Sal, I believed life would follow my dreams in a single red line across the landscape of my life. But God says, "We can make our plans, but the LORD determines our steps" (Prov. 16:9). We never really know how he's going to determine our steps. So we must stay open to changes in the plan. Then when the path stalls and we find we are on the wrong road, we can either change our plans the way Sal did, or we can continue traveling our preconceived route, believing that we can somehow overcome what we know to be wrong. The other alternative is to go back to New York and give up.

Sal backtracks and takes the man's advice. He begins again. He doesn't give up on the westward journey. The dream possessed him, instead of his possessing the dream. When we possess the dream, we want to shape it. But when we let the dream shape us, then we have the power of purpose. And the power of purpose will not live for the opinions of men. It is faith in an eternal picture. It's the power to step out of a boat, overcoming the lie of the familiar. Sure, Peter sank, but as George Morrison pointed out, he did so in familiar waters.[4] He took his eyes, ears, and attention off the Lord who directed his steps by saying, "Come."

Peter knew the lake as you know the ropes of your career. He was a fisherman. He had his favorite fishing hole. He knew the shallow parts; the deep ones too. He knew every inch of the lake. He knew it in waters both choppy and calm. He knew what a storm could do to a boat and its occupants. Even though it was four in the morning, and though the other disciples may have grabbed at the corners of his cloak to hold him back, warning, "You will drown out there!" Peter opened himself up to danger. He believed that he could overcome the odds and walk on water.

The saddest thing that can happen is for a person to believe the lie of the familiar. It is to stop believing in possibility. Dreams become reality when they possess us. If we could interview Peter today, he would probably say, "I don't know what came over me. I just knew I had to do it. To live without the experience would have been to live without a larger idea of God." The larger idea of God always invites us beyond the status quo. It is the pillar of fire, shining beyond our moment. To follow it is to step away from the lie of the familiar.

The minute Peter fell back into the lie of the familiar, he sank. He tried to shape his own faith and he sank. Anytime we try to shape God into our own image, we'll sink. We'll hear the voice of the familiar say, "You are going to sink. You are going to die. You are going to be lonely the rest of your life. You will never find a job you love, so settle for the lousy one you have. You are never going to have a happy marriage, so settle on the affection of your children. That's all the affection you'll ever get." When we listen to the lie of the familiar, it shapes us toward apathy. We become a rider in the boat, instead of a walker on the water. We play it safe. But when we play it safe, we never get a larger idea of God. Because anytime you try to shape and limit the dream, it turns into the lie of the familiar.

Most of us sit in the boat with the rest of the disciples, quietly resenting those who take risks. We love to watch them fall. After Peter was saved, maybe they said, "We told you so!" But it didn't matter to Peter. He believed there was life beyond the familiar. One failure would not hold him from pursuing the possibilities. Sure, he gurgled water. He swallowed half of the lake. But had he remained in the boat, he would have never known the hand of Christ.

Life can become a place of possibility in the midst of the storm. We may need to enlarge our idea of God. This might have been what God was doing with the children of Israel. He enlarged their view of him, giving them a cloud by day and a pillar of fire by night. He knew they'd followed a regimen so long that freedom without guidance would plant in their minds an idolatrous idea, an idea that would eventually become the image of a golden calf. They needed something beyond the familiar regime, and so do we. Left to ourselves, we turn life into a party around a golden calf. And where does that bring us?

God knows we need guidance, so he sent the Holy Spirit. He placed the flame of God's Spirit inside the believer. The discovery of this fire sometimes sidetracks us, but it doesn't have to be for long. If we ask for his guidance, he will give it. "If you sinful people know how to give good gifts to your children, how much more will your heavenly Father give the Holy Spirit to those who ask him" (Luke 11:13). To ask God for his guidance is to receive a larger view of God.

We needed a larger view of God during that winter when 121 inches of snow fell. As we loaded trucks until 4:00 a.m. and studied during the day, we needed something holy, something on fire, something that went beyond our routine lives. We needed something to take us beyond simply loading trucks to pay for a seminary education.

A Gun-blue Snowstorm

One night, as we drove through a fierce snowstorm to the UPS center, listening to a religious radio station—twenty-four hours of preaching— we got more than we expected. The sky lit up as if we were going through a tunnel dimly lit with a translucent orange glow. It was a camera flash, but it glowed for a full five minutes. We were marooned in a moment we couldn't get out of, like a time warp, going nowhere. It was a tunnel of dingy light, black at both ends. We were three would-be theologians caught in some type of vision, as if we were seeing angels ascending and descending with faces of fire.

It's like the scene from Denis Johnson's book *Jesus' Son,* where the main character stumbles into a drive-in theater in a "gun-blue" snowstorm, and "the only light visible was a streak of sunset flickering below the hem of the clouds.... On the farther side of the field, just beyond the curtains of snow, the sky was torn away and the angels were descending out of brilliant blue summer, their huge faces streaked with light and full of pity. The sight of them cut through my heart and down the knuckles of my spine...."[5] Ours was the same type of vision. Light split the darkness beyond our Honda Accord. We didn't see any angels, but we knew something happened that night that none of us cares to explain.

We did not talk ever about it, beyond that moment. Never did we mention it on future rides to UPS. There was something otherworldly about it, like walking into Ezekiel's wheel inside a wheel. "I looked, and I saw a windstorm coming out of the north—an immense cloud with flashing lightning and surrounded by brilliant light. The center of the fire looked like glowing metal...." (Ezek. 1:4 NIV). It had a certain *feeling* to it. Being a boy from Tennessee, I'd never been in a "gun-blue" snowstorm turned into translucent fire. One of us would-be theologians gave a scientific explanation—*thundersnow*. It's lightning during a heavy snowstorm. But I thought it had to be more than that. I wanted to believe that something holy happened that night. Something like a vision, a sign that somehow we were traveling in his light, in his will, that it was a pillar of fire. You wonder when you go to seminary whether it's really God's will for you to be there, especially when you have to load a semi during the graveyard shift just to make ends meet. You need a sign, a pillar of fire, even if it's *thundersnow*. God knew what the children of Israel needed. "The LORD guided them by a pillar of cloud during the day and a pillar of fire at night. That way they could travel whether it was day or night" (Exod. 13:21). As A. W. Pink wrote, "In like manner, the Holy Spirit has been given to Christians to direct their steps along the Narrow Way which [leads] unto life."[6] "For all who are led by the Spirit of God are children of God" (Rom. 8:14). And the Holy Spirit's fire is what we all want guiding us. Once we find it, we have to follow. And following is hard for us. We make our plans and ask God to bless them. When he doesn't, we stumble into the darkness. Remember, life is a combination of the bitter and the sweet—triumphs and trials. And after the bitter waters of some trial, we often discover spiritual peace.

Which Way Is Your Pittsburgh?

Sal Paradise needed a new beginning. The stretch of Route 6 he'd chosen to begin his journey had no traffic. This meant he would not be able to hitchhike, and his travel plans depended on an outstretched thumb. It was a "northernmost hang-up." Goal blocked. California dream stalled. In this moment, he had a crisis. Richard Leider, in *The Power of Purpose,* gathered it together for us. It is "often in the midst of a crisis that we pull back from the entanglements of daily survival and let life question us. The benefit of a crisis is often the letting go of petty concerns, conflicts, and the need for control and the realization that life is short and every moment precious."[7]

As for Sal, his northernmost hang-up became a crisis. He had to backtrack to New York and then head to Pittsburgh. That's what repentance does. It backtracks. I'm not talking about repentance that leads to salvation, but repentance in our thinking. We change our thoughts and make a U-turn. We head for New York, so we can get to our new destination of Pittsburgh. We have to ask ourselves, "What is my destination? Where do I need to go next?"

Buechner wrote, "To Isaiah, the voice said, 'Go,' and for each of us there are many voices that say it, but the question is, which one will we obey with our lives.... I believe that it is possible to say at least this in general to all of us: we should go with our lives where we most need to go and where we are most needed."[8]

Wading Through Bitter Waters

The translucent orange glow we experienced as we headed for the UPS center in northern Massachusetts was the closest thing to a vision I've ever seen. It was eerie and somehow holy—a confirmation of God's presence that he'd take care of fools and seminary students in their late thirties. At that time Jill was at home in Tennessee. I was there by myself for four long months without her. I had the furniture. She had our two daughters. She longed to be with me, to leave my mother's home, to go north. She's a good woman. She'd proven she'd follow me anywhere, even to the land of 121 inches of snow. She understands sacrifices have to be made. If anything, we were obedient to the voice of God.

To exercise faith is to obey, just as Abraham did. It's to go searching for a city whose builder and maker is God. It's to come aside and

hear the voice of God in a burning bush. Because "Obedience is far better than sacrifice. Listening to him is much better than offering the fat
of rams" (I Sam. 15:22). We obeyed the voice of God that winter,
when it snowed 121 inches in the Boston area. We had wondered if we
really could trust his voice. Could we leave behind everything? Could
we cross over the Jabbok like Jacob? "... during the night Jacob got up
and sent his two wives, two concubines, and eleven sons across the
Jabbok River. After they were on the other side, he sent over all his pos-
sessions. This left Jacob all alone in the camp, and a man came and
wrestled with him until dawn" (Gen. 32:22–24). That long winter in
Boston was when I wrestled with an angel. I smashed my finger at UPS
after a box fell on it. The nail turned purple and started throbbing. It
throbbed for two days before Bruce, my buddy across the hall, sat me
down at his kitchen table and drilled it with a borrowed drill bit from
the maintenance shop in married housing. He twisted it for more than
five minutes with me protesting all the way. "How do you know this
will relieve the throbbing?" On and on, until we finally struck oil. It
spurted past Bruce onto the table.

"Whoa, baby!" he said.

Then we laughed.

Then I hurt my back at UPS and couldn't get out of bed. Bruce
came over, lifted me out of bed, and carried me to the doctor. That
place north of Boston turned out to be a northernmost hang-up, a
place I would soon leave. Just like Sal Paradise, I traveled back to my
original starting point, only to start again. Wrong turns on the road are
never failures if you are willing to start again with your dream. The
dreams that possess us will never let us stay the same. Jeremiah knew
this. He understood the fire possessing him. "So these messages from
the LORD have made me a household joke. And I can't stop! If I say I'll
never mention the LORD or speak in his name, his word burns in my
heart like a fire. It's like a fire in my bones! I am weary of holding it in!"
(Jer. 20:8–9). I couldn't hold the fire inside.

Finding My Own Pittsburgh

I returned to Tennessee after the first semester. Jill's mother had a recurrence of breast cancer, and Jill wanted to be near her to care for her. Sacrifice sometimes accompanies obedience. We have to die to self daily by picking up our own crosses. My friend Bruce sacrificed for me. Without him, the winter it snowed 121 inches in the Boston area would have broken me. The fire dimmed, but Bruce helped keep it alive.

We really do need each other. Maybe that's the most important lesson I learned in seminary. I had to sell my home and most of our belongings to learn one simple lesson: We need each other. There it is: what I learned in seminary!

Bruce is a pastor somewhere in Connecticut. I haven't talked with him since that year, but maybe he tells stories about the southern aberration that darkened married couples' housing the winter it snowed 121 inches. Maybe he's talking about how he sat at his kitchen table and drilled my thumb to make the pain go away; how he healed a southern boy's finger; and how he got that boy out of bed when he hurt his back lifting boxes twice his size. Maybe he's telling them he watched me load my U-Haul truck in order to leave just as fast as I came. I wish I could tell him that I eventually completed my seminary training. I didn't give up. I just needed to go back. I needed to find my own Pittsburgh.

I transferred to Gordon-Conwell's extension campus in Charlotte and drove every month—seven hours one way—to each class that met one weekend a month for three months. It was my own Pittsburgh. I didn't give up! I only discovered God's plan in the roundabout way and through 121 inches of snow. I witnessed God's mysterious ways, like William Cowper, the great hymn writer who wrote "God Moves in Mysterious Ways."

It was late in the evening when Cowper wrote the hymn. A storm had bathed the streets and gurgled in the drains of a foggy London. And William Cowper was at a point of despair. He could not write. He had nothing but anguish in his pen. So he threw it down and stalked out of his house. He hailed a horse-drawn cab and asked to be taken to the Thames River. He planned to throw himself off the bridge to commit suicide. But the fog was so thick, the cabby could not find his way to the river. For two hours, he traveled in a haze and then drew up the horse and said, "Mr. Cowper, I can't find the way." Cowper stumbled out of the cab and realized to his astonishment that the cabby had been driving in circles. Cowper was in front of his own house, so he entered. He walked to his desk—where he had thrown down his pen in despair—and got on his knees to commit his life to God. Then he sat at his desk and wrote,

> God moves in a mysterious way
> His wonders to perform;
> He plants his footsteps in the sea,
> And rides upon the storm.
>
> Deep in unfathomable mines
> Of never-failing skill
> He treasures up his bright designs,
> And works his sovereign will.
>
> Ye fearful saints, fresh courage take,
> The clouds ye so much dread
> Are big with mercy, and shall break
> In blessings on your head.
>
> Judge not the Lord by feeble sense,
> But trust him for his grace;
> Behind a frowning providence
> He hides a smiling face.
>
> His purposes will ripen fast,
> Unfolding every hour;

The bud may have a bitter taste,
But sweet will be the flower.

Blind unbelief is sure to err,
And scan his work in vain;
God is his own interpreter,
And He will make it plain.

My trip to Gordon-Conwell in Massachusetts may have led me back to where I started, but I can say, as Cowper said, "God is his own interpreter, and He will make it plain." And God made my way plain as the driven snow. This is my prayer for you! May God make his mysterious sovereign will known.

Notes

Chapter One: One-Way Trip

1. Millard Erickson, *Christian Theology* (Grand Rapids, Mich.: Baker, 1983), 812.
2. Paul Tournier, *Guilt and Grace,* trans. Arthur W. Heathcote (New York: Harper & Row, 1962), 67.
3. Ibid., 10.
4. William James, *The Varieties of Religious Experience* (New York: Modern Library Edition, 1994), 61.
5. Mitch Albom, *The Five People You Meet in Heaven* (New York: Hyperion, 2003).
6. Tournier, 157.
7. Erickson, 821.
8. Hans Kung, *On Being Christian* (New York: Image Books, 1984), 585.
9. Frederick Buechner, *The Hungering Dark* (San Francisco: HarperSanFrancisco, 1985), 109.

Chapter Two: Blasting the Very Foundations of Christianity

1. C. S. Lewis, *Mere Christianity* (New York: Touchstone Books, 1996), 63.
2. An interview with John Walters, *Front Porch,* New Hampshire Public Radio, http://www.nhpr.org/view_content/4962/

3. You can read more about this in James Garlow and Peter Jones' book, *Cracking Da Vinci's Code* (Colorado Springs: Cook Communications, 2004).
4. Millard Erickson, *Christian Theology* (Grand Rapids, Mich.: Baker, 1983), 819.
5. Ibid., 820.
6. Lewis, 64.
7. Philip Yancey, *What's So Amazing About Grace?* (Grand Rapids, Mich.: Zondervan, 1997), 62.
8. Frederick Buechner, *The Magnificent Defeat* (New York: HarperCollins, 1966; Harper & Row, 1985), 47.

Chapter Three: Life at a Crossroads

1. Frederick W. Robertson, *Sermons Preached at Brighton* (New York: Harper & Brothers, n.d.), 434.
2. Malcolm Gladwell, "Listening to Khakis: What America's Most Popular Pants Tell Us about the Way Guys Think," *New Yorker,* 28 July 1997 http://www.gladwell.com/1997/1997_07_27_a_khaki.htm
3. C. P. Farley, "Author interviews: Chuck Palahniuk on Oprah's Diaphragm," Powells.com: http://www.powells.com/authors/palahniuk.html

Chapter Five: When Life's Demands Exceed Our Load Capacity

1. Erik Erikson, *Identity and the Life Cycle* (New York: W.W. Norton, 1980), 89.
2. Frederick Robertson, *Sermons Preached at Brighton* (New York: Harper & Brothers, n.d.), 809.
3. Larry Crabb, *Inside Out* (Colorado Springs: NavPress, 1991), 14.
4. Henri Nouwen, *Turn My Mourning into Dancing* (Nashville: W, 2001), 13.

5. Dr. Arthur Freeman and Rose DeWolf, *Woulda, Coulda, Shoulda* (New York: William Morrow, 1989; HarperPerennial, 1990), 54.

Chapter Six: The Strength and Patience to See It Through

1. Harry Emerson Fosdick, *Living Under Tension* (New York: Harper & Brothers, 1941), 206.
2. Erich Fromm, *To Have or To Be?*, Ruth Nanda Anshen, ed. (New York: Harper & Row, 1976), 5.
3. C. S. Lewis, *Mere Christianity*, (New York: Touchstone Books, 1996), 170.
4. Fosdick, 203.
5. Lewis, 54.
6. Ibid.

Chapter Seven: Watch Out for Falling Rocks and Flying Debris

1. Helmut Thielicke, *The Waiting Father: Sermons on the Parables of Jesus*, trans. John W. Doberstein (New York: Harper & Row, 1959), 87.
2. Ibid., 131–32.
3. Frederick Buechner, *The Alphabet of Grace* (San Francisco: HarperSanFrancisco, 1970), 25.

Chapter Eight: Staying Out of the Tow-Away Zone

1. Oswald Chambers, as quoted in Os Guinness, *God in the Dark* (Wheaton: Crossway, 1996), 63.
2. Leslie D. Weatherhead, *Salute to the Sufferer* (Nashville: Abingdon, 1962), 17, 19.
3. Charles Haddon Spurgeon, *The Treasury of David*, updated by Roy H. Clarke (Nashville: Nelson, 1997), 814.
4. George Buttrick, *Sermons Preached in a University Church* (New York: Abingdon, 1959), 41.
5. Ibid., 28.

Chapter Nine: Getting into Position Is Only Half of It

1. Martin E.P. Seligman, *Learned Optimism* (New York: Pocket Books, 1992; New York: A.A. Knopf, 1991), 4.
2. Os Guinness, *God in the Dark* (Wheaton: Crossway Books, 1996), 213.
3. Dr. Arthur Freeman and Rose DeWolf, *Woulda, Coulda, Shoulda* (New York: William Morrow, 1989; HarperPerennial, 1990), 141.
4. William Barclay, *The Gospel of John*, vol. 1, rev. ed., The Daily Study Bible Series (Philadelphia: Westminster, 1975), 179.
5. George A. Gordon, "The World Under the Aspect of Tragedy," *Great Modern Sermons*, ed. Hobart D. McKeehan (New York: Revell, 1923), 73.
6. Helmut Thielicke, *How the World Began*, trans. John W. Doberstein (Philadelphia: Fortress Press, 1974), 251
7. Harry Emerson Fosdick, *Living Under Tension* (New York: Harper & Brothers, 1941), 102.
8. Thomas Merton, as quoted in Henri Nouwen, *Turn My Mourning into Dancing* (Nashville: W, 2001), 60.

Chapter Ten: Evacuation Route

1. Henri Nouwen, *Turn My Mourning into Dancing* (Nashville: W, 2001), 56.
2. Ibid., 60.
3. Thomas Merton, *Life and Holiness* (New York: Herder & Herder, 1963), 21.

Chapter Eleven: Keep Off!

1. C. S. Lewis, *The Problem of Pain* (New York: Simon & Schuster, 1996; reprint, New York: Macmillan, 1962), 36.
2. Luke 9:54.
3. John Calvin, as quoted in Dallas Willard, *The Divine Conspiracy* (San Francisco: HarperSanFrancisco, 1997), 21.

4. William Barclay, *The Gospel of Luke*, rev. ed. (Philadelphia: Westminster, 1975),

5. C. S. Lewis, *The Problem of Pain* (New York: Touchstone Books, 1996), 103.

6. John Nolland, *Word Biblical Commentary: Luke 9:21–18:34*, vol. 35B, ed. Ralph P. Martin (Dallas: Word, 1993), 537.

Chapter Twelve: Watch Out for the Added Lane

1. Charles Haddon Spurgeon, *The Treasury of David*, updated by Roy H. Clarke (Nashville: Nelson, 1997), 1176.

2. William Barclay, *The Letters of James and Peter*, rev. ed. (Philadelphia: Westminster, 1976), 342.

3. Dr. Arthur Freeman and Rose DeWolf, *Woulda, Coulda, Shoulda* (New York: William Morrow, 1989; HarperPerennial, 1990), 157.

4. Flannery O'Connor, *Mystery and Manners* (New York: Noonday Press, 1997; Farrar, Straus and Giroux, 1969), 48.

5. Barclay, *The Letters of James and Peter*, 342.

6. Frederick Buechner, *The Longing for Home* (San Francisco: HarperSanFrancisco, 1996), 109.

7. Frederick Buechner, *The Hungering Dark* (San Francisco: HarperSanFrancisco, 1985), 78–9.

Chapter Thirteen: The Bump in Every Road

1. Robert B. Ewen, *An Introduction to Theories of Personalities*, 4th ed. (Hillsdale, N.J.: Lawrence Erlbaum Associates, 1993), 92.

2. George Buttrick, *The Parables of Jesus* (New York: Harper & Brothers, 1928), 73.

3. Ewen, 92.

4. C. S. Lewis, *Mere Christianity* (New York: Touchstone Books, 1996), 87.

5. Ibid., 71.

6. Harry Emerson Fosdick, *Living Under Tension* (New York: Harper & Brothers, 1941), 109.
7. Ibid.
8. Ibid., 110.
9. Lewis, 170.
10. Frederick Buechner, *The Eyes of the Heart* (New York: HarperCollins, 1999), 182.
11. Fosdick, 55.

Chapter Fourteen: The Life You Save May Be Your Own

1. Dennis D. Morgan, *Life in Process* (Wheaton: Victor, 1993), 25.
2. Dr. Arthur Freeman and Rose DeWolf, *Woulda, Coulda, Shoulda* (New York: William Morrow, 1989; HarperPerennial, 1990), 59.

Chapter Fifteen: The Northernmost Hang-up

1. Jack Kerouac, *On the Road* (New York: Penguin, 1999), 9.
2. Ibid.
3. Ibid.
4. George H. Morrison, *Wind on the Hearth: The Morrison Classic Library* (Grand Rapids, Mich.: Kregel, 1994), 41.
5. Denis Johnson, *Jesus' Son* (New York: HarperPerennial, 1993), 81.
6. Arthur W. Pink, *Gleanings in Exodus* (Chicago: Moody Press, 1973), 105.
7. Richard J. Leider, *The Power of Purpose* (San Francisco: Berrett-Koehler Publishers, 1997), 13–14.
8. Frederick Buechner, *The Hungering Dark* (New York: HarperCollins, 1969; Harper & Row, 1985), 31.

READERS' GUIDE

For Personal Reflection
or Group Discussion

INTRODUCTION

Life is a journey littered with crossroads. And at every one, a question must be answered: "Which way do I go?" And, of course, there are other obstacles that hinder our progress to the next crossroads, making us ask, "God, how much longer?" We want the journey to culminate in a happy oasis away from the dusty streets of life. But God always answers our travel questions by saying, "Be patient. Not yet." And the realization that we will never arrive in this life can make journeying through it seem meaningless. We don't see instant results for our faith and obedience. But when we travel with eternity as our goal, we find peace and patience for this journey. As you look back over the principles applied in this book, think about how your present circumstances can be transformed. First, look upon your trials as being temporary in the big picture of eternity. It will help you differentiate between what is important for eternity and what's not, which will produce patience. Second, by using this readers' guide you'll be able to reflect on each road sign at critical crossroads. This will help you concentrate on areas of your life that need to be submitted to the process found in Romans 5:3–5: "We can rejoice, too, when we run into problems and trials, for we know that they are good for us—they help us learn to endure. And endurance develops strength of character in us, and character strengthens our confident expectation of salvation. And this expectation will not disappoint us." Enjoy the journey through this readers' guide.

READERS' GUIDE

Chapter 1
ONE-WAY TRIP

1. The author wrote that true guilt is "the conviction we feel after committing a sin.... It has to do with divine judgment. We step away from God's way, and we suffer the consequences.... [W]e repent, and then experience forgiveness." What is conviction? How does it feel?

2. "Then there's false guilt. [It is] the 'result of the judgments and suggestions of men.' It's the 'fear of taboos or of losing the love of others,' because of inferiority or poor performance." According to the author, what is false guilt? How would you define it? Give an example of how false guilt has worked in your life. Is there someone in your life that likes to put you on a guilt trip?

3. "Childhood guilt works like the fear of stepping on a crack to break your mother's back. It involves a sense of shame, a sense of wanting to please parents and family members." Mark an X on

the scale indicating how much you live to please others, instead of God.

Always   Sometimes   Never

4. Is seeking the approval of others a bad thing?

Read Genesis 3:9–10.
5. Did Adam and Eve hide because they felt conviction or false guilt?

Group Prayer Suggestion
Take time to pray for your group members who feel an intense sense of guilt. Comfort them with God's forgiveness.

Chapter 2
BLASTING THE VERY FOUNDATIONS OF CHRISTIANITY

1. C. S. Lewis wrote, "Ninety-nine per cent of the things you believe are believed on authority. I believe there is such a place as New York. I have not seen it myself. I could not prove by abstract reasoning that there must be such a place. I believe it because reliable people have told me so." Do you agree with Lewis? Is everything we believe a "leap of faith"? Is a "leap of faith" a bad thing? Can we and must we know everything about something to believe in it?

2. Dan Brown, of *Da Vinci Code* fame, believes that before Constantine, the church fathers all believed that Christ was a mortal man, that Christ is not divine, but only a prophet. Do you believe Christ was God in the flesh, or do you believe he was only a prophet? Will choosing one over the other make a difference in our faith in God?

3. Reread the illustration of the firefighter on page 27. Is this a good analogy about how Christ saves our lives? Why?
4. What are the consequences if Dan Brown is right about Jesus being only a great teacher without divinity?

Read Romans 5:9.
5. How does the blood of Christ cleanse us from sin?

Group Prayer Suggestion
Take time to pray for your group members who feel confused about Jesus' divinity. Comfort them with the fact that God has given his all by sending his Son to die for our sins.

 *Chapter 3*
LIFE AT A CROSSROADS

Read Mark 14:32–42.
1. Why do you think the disciples fell asleep in the Garden of Gethsemane? Can emotions play into our spiritual life? Were the disciples tired or spiritually inept?

2. The author says the subtle battle we overlook is to remain awake in moments of significance. Have you ever been so distracted by worry about work, the bills, or the church social that you missed an important moment in the life of your children, spouse, or other loved one? Maybe you were present in their Garden of Gethsemane, but you weren't attentive to their needs.

3. Chuck Palahniuk, author of *Fight Club*, discussed the idea that everyone has a passion, and the reason we don't find it is because we've talked ourselves out of it. Have you ever talked

yourself out of making a career change or another needed change in your life? What was the result?

4. Chuck Palahniuk sums up passion in this saying: "Don't push the river, it flows." What does that mean?

Group Prayer Suggestion

Take prayer requests from the members of your group who desire change but don't know how to implement the process of change.

Chapter 4
WHAT'S AROUND THE CORNER?

1. The author wrote, "Sometimes we make the trade for a lucky rabbit's foot. We love to fret, so we trade the peace of God for it. We love to hold grudges, so we trade God's love for it. We love to lust, so we trade purity for it." Have you traded a gift of God (peace, love, purity, and so forth) for a lucky rabbit's foot? Are you holding a grudge? If yes, what has this grudge robbed you of?

2. Billy shoved a sheet of paper under the door, seeking Robert's forgiveness. Have you ever slipped a piece of paper underneath God's door? If so, how did this affect your life? Is there anyone in your life, besides God, who deserves a note of apology or forgiveness slipped under his or her door?

Read Hebrews 12:16–17.
3. Esau traded his birthright for stew. How did that affect his relationship with God? How does our trading the things of God for the things of this world affect our relationship with God? Is it possible to have the things of the world and the things of God at the same time? If not, why not?

Read Isaiah 64:6.

4.   The author wrote, "God spoke through a twelve-year-old and said, 'Robbie, when will you ever learn: I love your broken heart before me more than what you have in your hand. All of your righteousness is like the broken arm of a figurine. It's a coat from a secondhand store.'" Is the author right about our righteousness being like a broken arm of a figurine? Why?

5.   If we have no righteousness, what makes us good enough in God's eyes? How good do we have to be?

Group Prayer Suggestion

Pray for those in your group who feel they don't measure up. Assure them of Christ's role in our righteousness.

Chapter 5

WHEN LIFE'S DEMANDS EXCEED OUR LOAD CAPACITY

1.   How has the author's view of crying invaded your life? Do you believe "big boys don't cry"? Why does our culture believe crying is a sign of weakness?

2.   Mark Twain said the death of a loved one is like when your house burns down; it isn't for years that you realize the full extent of your loss. Do you agree? Why or why not?

Read Psalm 126:5.

3.   Do you believe that those who sow in tears will reap with songs of joy? What do you believe the psalmist meant? Is this possible?

4. Erik Erikson said we emerge from sorrow by restoring our sense of mastery, which takes place as "we repeat, in ruminations and in endless talk ... experiences that have been too much for us." Do you believe talking about someone's death or memory helps a grieving person get over sorrow? Is this good or bad?

Read Matthew 11:28.

5. How does Jesus take our burdens away? Is it an exchange of our strength for his? Mark an X on the scale below indicating how often you allow Christ to carry your burdens.

Always   Sometimes   Never

6. Give an example of a burden that you need to give to God.

Group Prayer Suggestion

Take time to pray for your group members' burdens. Read to them this Scripture verse: "Don't worry about anything; instead, pray about everything. Tell God what you need, and thank him for all he has done" (Philippians 4:6).

 *Chapter 6*

THE STRENGTH AND PATIENCE TO SEE IT THROUGH

1. Have you ever started a diet or training program or any other health management exercise and quit? Why do you think we are more likely to quit than to succeed?

2. The author asked, "Are we going to allow our schedules to shape our lives, or are we going to allow our lives to dictate our schedules? We can do anything but not everything." Can our

schedules shape our lives? If so, is this good or bad? How can we maintain balance in life? Do we control this balance?

Read Matthew 16:26.

3. C. S. Lewis wrote that we are all "trying to let our mind and heart go their own way—centered on money or pleasure or ambition—and hoping, in spite of this, to behave honestly and chastely and humbly." Do you believe this describes the way you live? If so, why? If not, how have you overcome this subtle trap?

4. The author wrote, "Discipline from within is the one true way, because discipline forced on us from without usually makes us into frauds. We learn to do as the Pharisees did. They faked it when they didn't have the inner strength or the desire to follow God with their whole hearts." How does faking a relationship with God do one of the following:

   Produce guilt
   Damage relationship with others
   Affect the way we view discipline

Read Matthew 6:24.

5. C. S. Lewis wrote, "Now God designed the human machine to run on himself. He himself is the fuel our spirits were designed to burn, or the food our spirits were designed to feed on." Lewis went on to say that when we run our lives on human strength it's the wrong juice. Describe the difference between the wrong juice and the right juice. How can you operate your life on the correct fuel?

Group Prayer Suggestion

Pray for God to give your group members the courage to maintain balance in their relationships with Christ and for the discipline needed to improve their lives.

Chapter 7

WATCH OUT FOR FALLING ROCKS AND FLYING DEBRIS

Read 1 Peter 2:11–15.
1. How should a Christian be different from the world? Is it a matter of following dos and don'ts? Or is it a matter of the heart? What motivates us to be strangers in this world?

Read Luke 18:9-14.
2. Why did Jesus condemn the Pharisee? What did Jesus not like about him?

3. Why did Jesus approve of the publican? Do you feel closer to the Pharisee or the tax collector? How much closer to God are those who "stand at a distance" than those who sit in the pews?

4. Helmut Thielicke said the Pharisee "measures himself by looking downward when he tries to determine his rank before God.... this kind of self-measurement by looking downward always produces pride." Have you ever measured your spirituality by comparing yourself to others? Why do we do this?

5. The author wrote, "Why do we feel so compelled to earn our way? Is it because we feel grace is a one-shot deal, and every sin after our initial repentance remains outstanding?" How would you answer this question? Do you ever feel as if some of your sins are unforgivable? Explain.

Group Prayer Suggestion

Take some time to pray for honesty in your relationship with God. Pray for God to show you the blind spots of pharisaical tendencies.

Chapter 8
Staying Out of the Tow-Away Zone

1. Have you ever doubted God's goodness? Explain.

Read Psalm 91:9-11.
2. Do we misunderstand God's protection? Is God two-faced in a world that is known for its righteousness and evil? Does God offer false hope?

3. Leslie Weatherhead wrote, "[God] *allows* human sin, or man would have no real free will. He does not will or intend sin. God is responsible for its possibility, not for its actuality...." How is God responsible for the possibility of sin? What is free will? Do we have a choice in what happens to us?

Read Psalm 91.
4. Spurgeon wrote, "It is impossible for any ill to happen to those who are the Lord's beloved. The most crushing calamities can only shorten the journey and hasten their reward. To them, ill is no ill, only good in a mysterious form." Do you believe this statement? Should we see heaven as the ultimate reward, rather than seeking happiness at all costs in this world?

Group Prayer Suggestion
Take some time to pray for those who are feeling despair and doubt. Then pair up with someone in your group and pray for your partner every day this week.

Chapter 9
GETTING INTO POSITION IS ONLY HALF OF IT

Read John 5:2-9.

1. The author wrote about the man by the pool in John 5, "He may have asked, 'God, how much longer?' but he never turned it into an accusation. Bitterness was not in him. It takes character to persevere for thirty-eight years." How did this man persevere for thirty-eight years? Could you do what he did, if you were in his situation? How does your situation differ from his?

Read Romans 5:2-5.

2. Psychologist Martin Seligman wrote, "People who give up easily believe the causes of the bad events that happen to them are permanent." Do you believe this? If no, why? If yes, explain.

3. The author refers to the children's song "The Itsy-Bitsy Spider." On the graph below, put an X indicating what you would do if you were the itsy-bitsy spider.

├────┼────┼────┼────┼────┼────┼────┼────┤

| *Keep climbing* | *Try a few times* | *Quit after the* |
| *no matter what* | *then quit* | *initial try* |

4. How are you going to get up the spout? What will you do if the water washes you out? How does this transfer to your own life?

5. The author wrote, "Impatience asks the question, How much longer? It really doesn't believe God has a plan. But God's plan is not a matter of *if*, but *when*." Do you believe this? If so, how how has or could it change your perspective on life?

6. Jesus asked the man, "Do you want to be made well?" Why do

you think Jesus asked this question? Was it because he knew the man would have to get a job and so forth? Have you ever felt God was asking you this question? How did it change your future?

Group Prayer Suggestion

Take some time to pray for those who need the courage to persevere in their trial. Then for the next week, see yourself as the itsy-bitsy spider that never quits no matter what.

Chapter 10
EVACUATION ROUTE

Read Acts 15:36-41.

1. The author wrote, "All of us have played our part in revenge. We've hated. We've refused to offer forgiveness. We've sinned willingly. We've written someone off as the apostle Paul wrote off John Mark at the beginning of the second missionary journey." Do you think Paul should have allowed John Mark to travel with them on the second missionary journey even though he deserted them on the first?

2. The author wrote, "Was Barnabas a pushover, lacking discipline?" Was he enabling John Mark or offering forgiveness?

3. Is there someone in your family or at your workplace in need of your patience? How can you allow for the slow process of growth?

4. The author wrote, "Our wayward loved ones need second chances with tough love." What does it mean to give a second chance with tough love? Have you ever had to use tough love? What was the result?

Read 2 Thessalonians 1:3.

5. Thomas Merton wrote, "[Holiness] is not a matter of being *less* human, but *more* human than other men. This implies a greater capacity for concern, for suffering, for understanding, for sympathy, and also for humor, for joy, for appreciation of the good and beautiful things of life." Are you growing in love and concern for others? How does becoming more human give us greater capacity for concern?

Read Matthew 18:3.

6. What does it mean to become like little children? Why does Jesus make this comment?

Group Prayer Suggestion

Take some time to pray for wayward loved ones who need second chances with tough love.

 *Chapter 11*

KEEP OFF!

1. In what circumstances have you asked God to do for you what you didn't have the guts to do for yourself? Have you ever thought of God as being the grandfather in the sky? Explain.

Read Luke 9:54.

2. Do you think James and John were in the wrong when they lashed out at those who would not let Jesus have a room for the night? Have someone in your group be the hotel manager and two others be James and John. Act out the confrontation. Then have James and John report to the group what just took place. How many in the group agree with James and John's report? How many disagree? If you were Jesus, how would you respond to them?

3.   The author wrote, "When we stop to ask ourselves what spirit we are of, it changes the way we relate to the world." How many times during the day do you think before you act? What would happen if we asked this question before acting? Would it make a difference?

4.   Do you believe a selfish pursuit for happiness demands happiness on our terms? Why? Will God always give us what makes us happy? Why or why not? Give an example from your life when God has not given you what you thought would make you happy.

5.   The author wrote, "The eyes of love are tolerant. The right spirit fixes its eyes on the big picture, which for James and John should have been the crucifixion that was about to take place in Jerusalem." Do you ever lose sight of the big picture of one day being with Christ in heaven? Why do we lose it? When have you allowed circumstances to rob you of the larger picture? How did you refocus?

Group Prayer Suggestion

Take time to pray for each person to keep his or her eyes on the larger picture. Pray this verse for the group: "[We] lift up [our] eyes to you, to you whose throne is in heaven" (Ps. 123:1 NIV).

 *Chapter 12*
WATCH OUT FOR THE ADDED LANE

Read Psalm 119:105.
1.   Spurgeon said of the lamp in Psalm 119:105, "Having no fixed lamps in certain ancient towns, each person carried a lantern to avoid falling into the open sewer or stumbling over the heaps of manure that defiled the road. This is a true picture of our path

through this dark world." How is this a true picture of traveling through this world?

2. The author wrote, "Crossroads are restless moments, a time of movement, where our feet have to go in some direction, even when we don't know where to step." Which crossroads in your life have been most significant? How did you make the choice at the crossroads?

Read 2 Peter 3:8-9.

3. The author wrote, "Time does not control God, and this is hard for us to comprehend and accept. We are dawdlers who lose blocks of time and accuse God of stealing them. We think he is slow. We wish he moved according to our schedule. But God will not get involved in time. He is above it." Why do you think God is not bound by time? Why do you think we are?

4. Can we live on eternal time in this life? If so, how would it change life for us?

Group Prayer Suggestion

Take time to pray for your group members who feel that their lives are at a crossroads. Pray for God to give them light on their paths.

 *Chapter 13*

THE BUMP IN EVERY ROAD

1. The author wrote, "The goal is to become, not an individualized self, but more Christlike. The objective is to build up what C. S. Lewis called the 'the central part of you.' The part of us that makes our 'life as a whole, with all your innumerable choices, all [our] life long [we] are slowly turning this central thing either into a heavenly creature or into a hellish creature....'" Do you agree with Lewis that we have a central part that is turning either

heavenly or hellish? If so, how does this work? Is it like the analogy of the black dog and the white dog, and whichever one we feed is the one that grows and takes over?

Read Ephesians 4:21-23.

2. The author wrote, "Spiritual formation is not synonymous with salvation; it's not that we have a license to sin. Neither does it consist of working our way to heaven. Spiritual formation is, instead, a process whereby we work to bring our 'hidden things' into Christ's light." How can we work to bring hidden things into Christ's light? What's the difference between spiritual formation and trying to work your way into heaven?

3. Augustine said we should pray as if everything depended on God and work as if everything depended on us. Do you agree or disagree? Can you point out a verse in the Bible to support your view?

4. The author wrote, "Looking back, I can see it written all over the Indians fan's face. There was a strategy to his madness. But his means determined his end. It cost him." Do you believe that your means determines your end? How does this work? Give an example from your own life.

Group Prayer Suggestion

Pray for each member of your group to have the strength and the resolve to become Christlike in character.

 *Chapter 14*

THE LIFE YOU SAVE MAY BE YOUR OWN

Read 2 Corinthians 10:5.

1. The author gave the analogy of a sticky-board as being like our

minds, where bad emotions can get stuck. He wrote, "Whatever is trapped on the sticky-board must be killed." How does this analogy line up with 2 Corinthians 10:5? Can we stop bad thoughts from entering our minds? If no, then how do we deal with them?

2. Dennis Morgan believes "emotions dictate the interpretation of every piece of information.... How we feel becomes more real than truth." Do you agree or disagree? Why? What part does emotion play inside a belief in God? Should a Christian ever get emotional? Can you be too emotional?

3. The author wrote, "When we attach *emotional reasoning* to God, it becomes a warped faith that makes excuses for our behavior. We say, 'Besides, God understands why I do this.'" Have you ever justified your sins? If yes, give an example or give an example of someone you know who does this.

Read 1 Corinthians 12:13.
4. The author wrote, "For twenty-five years, I carried around racial baggage, feeling uncomfortable when I was in the presence of an African-American." How does racial prejudice manifest itself in your church? Is there a dividing line? If so, how could you help break down this wall?

Read Matthew 6:10.
5. The author wrote, "Every thought during a crisis is subjected to this question: 'How would heaven respond to my situation?' How would I act if I were having this crisis in heaven?" Do you believe it is possible to live and do things on earth as they are in heaven? If so, how do we do this?

Group Prayer Suggestion
Take time to pray for those in your group who are struggling with bad thoughts such as worry, lust, doubt, and so forth. Reread 2

Corinthians 10:5, asking each member to spend time memorizing this verse.

Chapter 15
THE NORTHERNMOST HANG-UP

1. Have you ever been in a "northernmost hang-up," where you knew you were traveling the wrong way? What did you do to remedy the situation?

Read Matthew 14:22-36.
2. Why did Peter think he could walk on water? Would you attempt what Peter did? Why or why not?

3. The author wrote, "The saddest thing that can happen to a person is to believe the lie of the familiar. It is to stop believing in possibility." What is the lie of the familiar in your life? It could be a secure job you hate but are not willing to risk losing. How can you get a larger idea of God to help you believe in possibility?

4. Richard J. Leider said it is "... often in the midst of a crisis that we pull back from the entanglements of daily survival and let life question us. The benefit of a crisis is often the letting go of petty concerns, conflicts, and the need for control and the realization that life is short and every moment precious." Have you found this to be true? Have you experienced a crisis that caused you to do this? What was it?

Read I Samuel 15:22.
5. Why is obedience better than sacrifice? Are you prone more to obeying or to sacrificing? What if God said, "Rest," and someone at church asked you to join the choir? How would you respond? Would you sacrifice and join the choir? Or would you obey and

rest? Using this analogy, tell why obedience would be better than sacrifice.

6. Sal Paradise had to travel back to New York City, then head out to Pittsburgh to get free from his northernmost hang-up. What are you going to do to get free from your northernmost hang-up? What is your Pittsburgh? Where do you need to go from here?

Group Prayer Suggestion

Pray for God to show how to be free from your northernmost hang-up. Ask for clear direction and guidance. Then pray for the courage to follow your dreams.

The Word at Work Around the World

A vital part of Cook Communications Ministries is our international outreach, Cook Communications Ministries International (CCMI). Your purchase of this book, and of other books and Christian-growth products from Cook, enables CCMI to provide Bibles and Christian literature to people in more than 150 languages in 65 countries.

Cook Communications Ministries is a not-for-profit, self-supporting organization. Revenues from sales of our books, Bible curricula, and other church and home products not only fund our U.S. ministry, but also fund our CCMI ministry around the world. One hundred percent of donations to CCMI go to our international literature programs.

CCMI reaches out internationally in three ways:

· Our premier International Christian Publishing Institute (ICPI) trains leaders from nationally led publishing houses around the world.

· We provide literature for pastors, evangelists, and Christian workers in their national language.

· We reach people at risk—refugees, AIDS victims, street children, and famine victims—with God's Word.

Word Power, God's Power

Faith Kidz, RiverOak, Honor, Life Journey, Victor, NexGen — every time you purchase a book produced by Cook Communications Ministries, you not only meet a vital personal need in your life or in the life of someone you love, but you're also a part of ministering to José in Colombia, Humberto in Chile, Gousa in India, or Lidiane in Brazil. You help make it possible for a pastor in China, a child in Peru, or a mother in West Africa to enjoy a life-changing book. And because you helped, children and adults around the world are learning God's Word and walking in his ways.

Thank you for your partnership in helping to disciple the world. May God bless you with the power of his Word in your life.

For more information about our international ministries, visit www.ccmi.org.

Additional copies of this or other Life Journey books
are available wherever good books are sold.

∝

If you have enjoyed this book,
or if it has had an impact on your life,
we would like to hear from you.

Please contact us at:

LIFE JOURNEY BOOKS
Cook Communications Ministries, Dept. 201
4050 Lee Vance View
Colorado Springs, CO 80918

Or visit our Web site: www.cookministries.com